ADVENTURES OF HUCKLEBERRY FINN

NOTES

including
- *Life and Background*
- *General Plot Summary*
- *List of Characters*
- *Note on Chapter Titles*
- *Summaries and Commentaries*
- *Character Analyses*
- *Review Questions*
- *Selected Bibliography*

by
James L. Roberts, Ph.D.
Department of English
University of Nebraska

NEW EDITION

INCORPORATED

LINCOLN, NEBRASKA 68501

Editor

Gary Carey, M.A.
University of Colorado

Consulting Editor

James L. Roberts, Ph.D.
Department of English
University of Nebraska

Cliffs Notes, Inc.   Lincoln, Nebraska

CONTENTS

Huckleberry Finn Notes

LIFE AND BACKGROUND

As one of America's first and foremost realists and humorists, Mark Twain, the pen name of Samuel Langhorne Clemens, usually wrote about his own personal experiences and things he knew about from firsthand experience. The various characters in *Adventures of Huckleberry Finn* are based on types which Twain encountered both in his home town and while working as a riverboat pilot on the Mississippi River.

Twain was born in the little town of Florida, Missouri, on November 30, 1835, shortly after his family had moved there from Tennessee. When he was about four, the family moved again, this time to Hannibal, Missouri, a small town of about five hundred people, situated on the Mississippi River about eighty miles from St. Louis. Hannibal was dusty and quiet with large forests nearby which Twain knew as a child and which he uses in *Huck Finn* when Pap kidnaps Huck and hides out in the great forest. The steamboats which passed daily were the fascination of the town and became the subject matter of Twain's *Life on the Mississippi*. The town of Hannibal is immortalized as St. Petersburg in Twain's *The Adventures of Tom Sawyer*.

Twain's father was a lawyer by profession, but was only mildly successful. He was, however, a highly intelligent man who was a stern disciplinarian. Twain's mother, a southern belle in her youth, had a natural sense of humor, was emotional, and was known to be particularly fond of animals and unfortunate human beings. Although the family was not wealthy, Twain apparently had a happy childhood. Twain's father died when Twain was twelve years old and, for the next ten years, Twain was an apprentice printer and then a printer both in Hannibal and in New York City. Hoping to find his fortune, he conceived a wild scheme of making a fortune in South America. On a riverboat to

New Orleans, he met a famous riverboat pilot who promised to teach him the trade for five hundred dollars. After completing his training, Twain was a riverboat pilot for four years and, during this time, he became familiar with all of the towns along the Mississippi River which play such an important part in *Huck Finn*, and he also became acquainted with every type of character which inhabits his various novels, especially *Huck Finn*.

When the Civil War began, Twain's allegiance tended to be somewhat southern due to his southern heritage, but his brother Orion convinced him to go west on an expedition, a trip which became the subject matter of a later work, *Roughing It*. Even though some of his letters and accounts of traveling had been published, Twain actually launched his literary career with the short story "The Celebrated Jumping Frog of Calaveras County," published in 1865. This story brought him national attention, and he devoted the major portion of the rest of his life to literary endeavors. He died in 1910.

GENERAL PLOT SUMMARY

Huck Finn decides to tell his own story since the reader has already heard about him through a novel called *The Adventures of Tom Sawyer*. As the son of the town drunkard, Huck has had difficulty living with the Widow Douglas and her sister, Miss Watson, since both want to civilize him. He prefers the easy and free manner of living wild. When his father discovers that Huck has some money, Huck is kidnapped and held prisoner in a shack across the river. His father beats him so brutally that Huck decides that he must escape or else his father will kill him some day. He creates a plan whereby it will appear that he has been murdered and then he goes to Jackson's Island to hide.

On the island he discovers Jim, Miss Watson's runaway slave, and Huck promises to keep Jim's secret. Huck discovers that some men are coming to the island to search for Jim, and the two escape by floating down the Mississippi River on a raft they had earlier discovered. They plan to go to the Ohio River and travel north into free states. On the river, they feel free and easy as they travel during the night and hide during the day. One night, in a storm, they float past Cairo and, since the raft can't go upstream, they search for a canoe. Before they find one, a steamship runs into the raft.

Huck climbs ashore and finds himself being challenged by the Grangerford men who are having a feud with the Shepherdsons. Huck tells them that he is George Jackson and that he fell overboard off a steamboat. He stays with them until he witnesses the deaths of many people in an outbreak of the feud. In the meantime, Jim has been discovered and they return to the raft and escape from the feuding.

Down the river, two scoundrels make their way to the raft and call themselves a duke and a king. At one town along the river, the king and the duke put on a trumped-up show and gull the townspeople out of a large sum of money. Continuing down the river, the king and the duke discover that a Peter Wilks has just died and left a large sum of money to two brothers in England who are expected any day. The king and the duke imitate the brothers in order to rob the Wilks family of its inheritance. Huck, however, is sympathetic to one of the nieces and foils their plan. As they escape and head down the river, the king and the duke are desperate for money, so they sell Jim to Silas Phelps for ransom money.

Huck hides the raft and goes to the Phelps farm where he is immediately mistaken for Tom Sawyer, who is supposed to arrive the same day. Huck goes out to meet Tom and they decide that Huck will remain Tom, and Tom will pretend to be his brother Sid. After many fantastic and ridiculous plans are put into effect to free Jim, at the moment of escape Tom is shot in the leg and Jim has to give up his chance for freedom to help nurse Tom. After the episode, however, it is discovered that Jim was already freed by his owner, Miss Watson, just before she died. Huck decides to head out for new territory because he does not like civilized society.

LIST OF CHARACTERS

Huckleberry Finn

Son of the town drunkard and narrator of the novel.

Tom Sawyer

Huck's respectable friend who delights in fantastic schemes.

Widow Douglas

Huck's unofficial guardian who wants to civilize him.

Miss Watson

The widow's hypocritical sister who pretends to be very pious.

Jim

Miss Watson's slave whom she plans to sell down the river.

Aunt Polly

Tom's aunt who is also his guardian.

Jo Harper, Ben Rogers, and Tommy Barnes

Members of Tom Sawyer's gang.

Pap

Huck's brutal, drunken father.

Judge Thatcher

The kindly judge who invests money for Huck.

Mrs. Loftus

A town lady whom Huck visits dressed as a girl.

Jake Packard, Bill, and **Jim Turner**

Cutthroats whom Huck discovers on a ship that is sinking.

The Grangerfords

The family who adopts Huck for a while and who are feuding with the Shepherdsons.

The duke and the king

The two scoundrels who take over the raft for a while.

Boggs

An offensive drunkard in a small Arkansas town who is shot down in cold blood.

Colonel Sherburn

The man who shoots Boggs and who later turns away the mob by ridiculing them.

Buck Harkness

The man who tries to lead the mob against Colonel Sherburn.

Peter Wilks

A well-to-do businessman with relatives in England. He has recently died and the family is waiting for the arrival of his two brothers from England.

William and **Harvey Wilks**

The two brothers who arrive after the duke and king pretend to be them.

Mary Jane, Susan, and **Joanna**

Peter Wilks' nieces.

Dr. Robinson and **Levi Bell**

Two townspeople who see through the guise of the duke and the king.

Silas Phelps

The man who buys Jim for the ransom money.

Aunt Sally Phelps

Silas' wife, also Tom Sawyer's aunt.

NOTE ON CHAPTER TITLES

In the original edition of the novel, Twain did not give titles to the individual chapters. In later editions, however, he did include titles to the various chapters. The following list presents the title he assigned to each chapter:

Chapter I	I DISCOVER MOSES AND THE BULRUSHERS
Chapter II	OUR GANG'S DARK OATH
Chapter III	WE AMBUSCADE THE A-RABS
Chapter IV	THE HAIR-BALL ORACLE
Chapter V	PAP STARTS IN ON A NEW LIFE
Chapter VI	PAP STRUGGLES WITH THE DEATH ANGEL
Chapter VII	I FOOL PAP AND GET AWAY
Chapter VIII	I SPARE MISS WATSON'S JIM

SUMMARIES AND COMMENTARIES

"TWAIN'S INTRODUCTORY NOTE"

Although Twain wrote this novel from 1876 through 1883, he set the time back in the era of slavery about "forty to fifty years" earlier. In between the actual time of the novel and the composition, the Civil War had theoretically freed the slaves, but the status of the Negro had not been improved and they were still kept in a subservient position.

Twain warns his readers that they will be persecuted if they attempt "to find a motive . . . or a moral" in the novel. This ironic statement, then, calls attention to the fact that there is definitely a serious intent to this novel which was missing in the earlier *The Adventures of Tom Sawyer*. While both books deal with the escapades of youths, and while both books capture something of the lost world of the young adolescent, the latter book can be read on a much deeper level.

Even though *Huck Finn* can profitably be read by younger persons, the greatness and the depth of the novel can only be fully appreciated and understood by the perceptive adult. Only the mature reader can completely recognize the complexity of this work of art, the profound social message, the verisimilitude of characterization, the psychological depths, and the moral values found individually throughout the various chapters.

In these introductory remarks, Twain makes it clear that he is imitating several different types of dialect—even though to an unfamiliar ear, it is sometimes difficult to distinguish between them. However, one has only to read the dialect found in other "local color" writers to recognize the greatness of Twain's use of dialect. The dialect used by Johnson Jones Hooper or Joel Chandler Harris, for example, has become almost impossible to read. Yet Twain was so careful and yet so accurate that his dialect lends piquancy to the novel and does not interfere with reading.

Twain's use of dialect has also contributed to the reputation of the novel, helping to evoke comments such as Ernest Hemingway's that this novel is the beginning of American literature. The novel, with its precise location, its subject matter of slavery and freedom, its rather definite time, and its unique array of frontier people place it as a uniquely American work of art.

CHAPTER I

Summary

Huck Finn reminds the readers that he has already appeared in a book about Tom Sawyer called *The Adventures of Tom Sawyer*. This book was "made by Mr. Mark Twain, and he told the truth, mainly. There was things which he stretched, but mainly he told the truth." He reminds us that at the end of that book, he and Tom had found six thousand dollars apiece. Since then, the Widow Douglas has been trying to civilize Huck, and Judge Thatcher has invested the money for him, bringing a dollar a day in interest.

The widow's sister, Miss Watson, also lives in the house, and she is forever picking at Huck, trying to make him do things her way. Unlike the Widow Douglas, who is kind and patient with Huck, Miss Watson is sharp and nagging. Her insistent interference makes Huck resent home life and its restraints. They won't even let him smoke.

Huck is so disgusted with home life that he accidentally kills a spider, and he knows that this act is bound to bring bad luck to him. However, as he sits and smokes, he hears Tom Sawyer's secret call. Huck puts out the light, slides to the ground, and finds Tom waiting for him among the trees.

Commentary

The opening sentence of the novel connects Huck with his appearance in *The Adventures of Tom Sawyer*. But as Huck says, "it ain't no matter" if the reader has not read the earlier work. In other words, Twain is letting us know that this is not a serial continuation — this novel is a complete work of art in its own right, is self-contained, and is not dependent upon other works.

Furthermore, Huck himself is going to be the narrator of this book and, thus, the reader will see all the events as Huck reports them. This choice of a narrator will provide the reader with much of the basic humor. That is, Huck, as narrator, reports things directly and never comments much on them. He is not aware of many of the incongruous items which he reports, and his failure to see the incongruity contributes to our reading pleasure. For example, in this chapter he runs away, but Tom Sawyer tells him that if he will "go back to the widow and be respectable," then he can become one of Tom's gang of robbers. The contradiction between the terms "respectable" and "robber" is beyond Huck's comprehension, but is immediately funny to the reader. This type of straightforward reporting, and failure to see the incongruous elements while reporting factually, is the basis of much of Twain's humor.

Of the many themes which run throughout the novel, several are introduced in this first chapter. First, Huck mentions that the Widow Douglas wanted to "sivilize" him. In contrast, Huck wants to escape and be "free and satisfied." The conflict between society and the individual becomes a controlling theme as the novel develops, and is investigated on several different levels. Furthermore, the novel ends with Huck planning "to light out" for a different territory because Aunt Sally plans to "sivilize" him. In between these opening and closing remarks, Huck encounters varying aspects, attitudes, and restrictions of society and learns to prefer his own individual freedom. This idea will receive its dramatic climax when Huck decides to oppose the dictates of society and "go to hell" for the sake of his friendship with Jim.

The restriction of living with the Widow Douglas also introduces the idea of Huck's quest for freedom which will later be correlated with Jim's quest of freedom from slavery. This theme will also function on many levels as Huck and Jim begin their trip down the river in search of freedom.

In conjunction with the restrictive effects of civilization is Twain's subtle satire on the traditional concepts of religion. Huck sees Miss Watson's traditional view of "a pearly gate" concept of heaven as being essentially boring and restrictive. The Widow Douglas' view is somewhat more appealing, but Huck would prefer to go to a more exciting place. The concept of religion, in general, throughout the novel is attacked by Twain in various guises. Basically, a society which required its property (its slaves) to become practicing Christians is a contradiction of the tenets of Christianity. Slaves were sometimes referred to, ironically, as "baptized property." For Twain, the concept of slavery and the pious religious concepts of the southerners were the height of contradictory absurdity.

Another theme introduced in this first chapter is that of Huck's birth and rebirth. When he feels stifled or deadened by society, he escapes to become reborn again. And throughout the novel, Huck loses his identity, assumes different names (even Tom Sawyer's), arranges his own murder, and then, in turn, is reborn with new or different values.

Furthermore, each time that Huck escapes from some situation, the theme of his loneliness and isolation is often touched upon. In this first chapter, he says that "I felt so lonesome I most wished I was dead." Man's feeling of loneliness and isolation is a recurrent theme in the total works of Twain. In this novel, it is expressed by Huck's encounter with the vastness of the frontier, with the magnitude of the Mississippi River and with the formidable forests which surrounded the settlements.

This feeling of loneliness is also correlated with the superstitions which permeate the novel. Confronted with the vastness of their isolation, Huck, Jim, and other characters put great reliance on superstitions of one sort or another. These superstitions develop into an important motif as the novel develops. In this first chapter, Huck is horrified by the implications inherent in accidentally flipping a spider into a candle and immediately makes the proper signs to ward off any bad luck.

Finally, Twain's careful craftsmanship is fully illustrated in the seemingly casual manner in which he introduces most of his major themes in his first chapter. In the hands of a lesser author, the introduction of such a variety of thematic material could possibly become contrived or artificial, yet Twain presents each theme as an integral part of the narrative structure of this short, first chapter.

CHAPTERS II AND III

Summary

As Huck joins Tom Sawyer in the garden, he accidentally trips over a root and alerts Miss Watson's slave, Jim, to the fact that something unusual is happening. Jim sits down on the ground between Tom and Huck, and he would have discovered them if he had not gone to sleep. Tom then plays a trick on Jim—a trick which multiplies in size as Jim tells the story after he awakes. With each telling, the story becomes more fanciful until Jim becomes the most envied Negro in the village.

Tom and Huck meet some other boys, and Tom wants to organize a band of robbers. From the various "pirate-books and robber-books" that Tom has read, he binds the members of his gang together with a beautiful oath and then makes plans to "stop stages and carriages on the road, with masks on, and kill the people and take their watches and money." Tom also wants to kidnap people and then hold them for ransom, but nobody knows what a ransom is. It is almost daylight before Huck creeps back through his window with his new clothes "all greased up and clayey. . . ."

After receiving a scolding from Miss Watson, Huck is also instructed in religion by the old maid, but he can't make any sense out of her type of sermonizing. About this time, a drowned body has been found and many people think it is Huck's pap, but Huck knows that he couldn't be that lucky. Unfortunately, he knows that his father would show up again some day even though he hasn't been around for over a year.

For about a month, the boys play robbers until Huck and all the other boys resign, for, by then, they have neither robbed nor killed anyone "but only just pretended." The romantic Tom argues with the realistic Huck about the value of make-believe and the importance of magicians, "genies," and the like. Huck tests the theory of genies by getting an old lamp, rubbing it for hours, and making elaborate plans for the genie. But when no genies appear, he loses faith in it and also questions Tom Sawyer's assertions.

Commentary

Chapters II and III introduce the characters of Tom Sawyer and Jim, both of whom will function prominently in the rest of the novel. Jim is introduced as Miss Watson's Negro. Such a seemingly innocent fact carries in Twain a certain importance. In other words, why couldn't Jim belong to the Widow Douglas? Twain is continuing his subtle distinction between these two women. Miss Watson's religion is based upon a more superficial and restrictive system than is the Widow Douglas'. In contrast, the Widow Douglas would "talk about Providence in a way to make a boy's mouth water," whereas Miss Watson would then "take hold and knock it all down again." Thus, with the Widow Douglas being more of a humanist in her religion, it is more fitting for the narrow-minded, restrictive Miss Watson to *own* a slave. Also, Huck's offering of Miss Watson — and not the Widow Douglas — as a person to be killed if he violates the oath to the band of robbers is a further indication of the contrast between Huck's system of values and that of the old maid.

The introduction of Tom functions as a contrast to Huck Finn. The extravagant plans and games which Tom introduces contrast to the sensible, practical, and functional plans which Huck institutes. This contrast is seen in Huck's escape from Pap, and in all of his schemes along the river, and is finally brought to a climax when Tom reappears at the Phelps plantation and instigates his fantastic escape schemes.

In contrast to the personality of Huck, Tom Sawyer represents a type of conformity to society. He *does* leave five cents on the table for the candles which they "steal," whereas Huck will always "borrow" what he needs to complete any scheme and will usually justify it in some manner or another. This small fact lends credence to Huck's view that Tom Sawyer could not possibly help free a slave (at the end of the novel) because of Tom's respectability and conformity to the views of society.

Tom's oaths, his schemes, and his escapades are based upon books about romantic adventures which he has read. Whereas Huck is involved in real life, Tom functions only when he is imitating something which he has read in a book. Furthermore, both here and at the end of the novel, Twain is ridiculing various aspects of romantic fiction which were very popular during that time. All of Tom's plans are satiric takeoffs on such fiction as *The Arabian Nights*, Alexander Dumas' *The Count of Monte Cristo*, or Cervantes' *Don Quixote* and many more novels of fantastic adventures. Mainly, however, these fictional adventures function as a contrast to the realistic and believable experiences of Huck Finn.

The Mississippi River, which will take on increasing symbolic importance as the novel progresses, is introduced as being "awful still and grand." Ultimately, the river will become the controlling image and main structural device, but already this early in the novel, Twain suggests its power and grandeur.

Jim's adherence to superstition, particularly with witches and devils in Chapter II, continues the superstition motif of the first chapter. Throughout the novel, Jim will often attribute their misfortunes to some type of bad luck sign, especially the snake bite in a subsequent chapter.

Through Huck Finn, Twain continues his gentle satire against religion. Twain himself had undergone serious contemplations about the nature of religion and the implications of religious faith, which receive their fullest expression in *The Mysterious Stranger,* published posthumously in 1916. Here, however, his satire is mild and is directed at religious sentimentality and superficiality. Huck's attempts to pray in order to get some fish hooks can hardly be viewed as a bitter attack on religion.

Huck's literal belief both in praying for fish hooks and in finding a genie in an old lamp illustrates again his literal minded-ness. This literal mindedness is a quality which will allow Huck to recognize Jim's basic qualities later on. That is, Huck accepts everything at face value and is not influenced by the values of society, as is Tom Sawyer. Huck's reliance upon the face value of an object then allows him to formulate his own system of values.

CHAPTERS IV AND V

Summary

After three or four months, during which time he attends school and learns to read and write, Huck sees some signs which suggest that his pap is back in town. Fearing his pap, he goes to Judge Thatcher and asks if there is any money from the invest-ments. The judge tells him the amount, and Huck wants to give it to the judge. Leaving the judge confused, Huck goes to have Jim consult his hair-ball to discover Huck's fortune. Huck's fears of his father's return are justified because that night when he went to his room, "there set pap, his own self!"

Pap stands before Huck looking vicious and mean. He curses Huck out for trying to get some education, for wearing nice clothes, and for the possibility that someday he might want to get some religion. He will not tolerate the idea of his son improv-ing himself and trying to be better than his own father. He forces Huck to give him the dollar which he had gotten from Judge Thatcher and goes to get some whiskey with it. He tries to bully Judge Thatcher into giving him the rest of Huck's money, but the judge refuses. He then goes to court to get custody of Huck, and even though the Widow Douglas and the judge oppose it, a new judge gives the custody of the boy to his father. Pap promises to reform with the aid of the new judge, but the improvement is short lived. Soon Pap trades his new coat for a jug of whiskey, gets drunk, rolls off the porch, and breaks his left arm in two places. The new judge gives up on Pap.

Commentary

The superstition motif is continued in Chapter IV and leads to Huck's fears that Pap is coming back. Spilling the salt leads to the discovery of the "cross in the left boot-heel" which Huck associates with his pap. Huck's fears impel him to rely upon Jim's knowledge of the occult. Beneath this scene is the gentle ridicule of superstition and magic; yet, Huck's fears are realized when he discovers his pap in the room at night.

When he first suspects that Pap has returned, Huck's immediate action is to try to give all his money to Judge Thatcher so that he won't be persecuted by his father. This is our first realization of Huck's perception and his shrewdness; that is, he knows that his pap will leave him alone if he has no money and since he dreads an encounter with his pap, he tries to give away the money so that he won't have to lie. This is not to imply that Huck objects to lying, but, in this case, it is the easiest course to follow because then he can convince his father that he has no money. Furthermore, Huck knows, as we later find out, that legally, a father has a right to any of his son's possessions. So, in one sense, Huck may be protecting his investment since he trusts the judge but not his own father.

Huck's willingness to part with such a large sum of money indicates his reliance upon other values and upon his own ability. Later, small sums seem much more important than such large abstract sums. This also suggests that Huck has not yet developed society's acquisitiveness.

In the depiction of Huck's pap, we have one of a series of superior characterizations of a minor character. Throughout the novel, Twain is able to depict so many of the secondary characters with such skill that they become memorable characters.

The introduction of Pap and his characterization indicate that Pap is a part of that society from which Huck wishes to escape. In contrast to Miss Watson's hypocrisy, Pap represents the brutality and severity of civilization which threaten to destroy Huck. Later we find that civilization is not as concerned over Huck's suffering at the hands of his pap as it is over discovering and rescuing Huck's dead body.

Unlike the American dream in which the parents desire something better for their children, Pap reprimands Huck for being able to read and write and climaxes his reprimand by asserting "First you know you'll get religion, too." More important is the reverse irony here. On a basic level, Pap is wrong because all children should learn to read and write, but, in the larger sense, we, the readers, do not want Huck to get educated in terms of the values of a society which advocates slavery, and we do not want him to adopt the type of religion which Miss Watson practices. Thus, on one level, Pap is wrong, but on a greater level, unknown to him, he is right.

The appearance of Pap prepares us for Huck's need to escape from a society which forces a son to obey such a thoroughly corrupt and evil person as Pap. The lack of understanding in the "new judge" when he refuses to "take a child away from its father" is another example of how society follows the old stereotyped concepts without considering the individual factors in the case. Only when the new judge sees personally the hypocrisy of Pap does he realize his error.

CHAPTERS VI AND VII

Summary

Huck is now determined to continue with his schooling, partly to spite his pap, who thrashes Huck every time he can catch him. When Pap hangs around the Widow Douglas' house too much, she threatens him. To get even with her, he kidnaps Huck and takes him across the river to a cabin in the woods where he keeps Huck locked up every time he leaves. Soon Huck gets used to living in the woods and has no desire to return to the widow and "sivilization."

The worse thing about living in the woods is that Pap beats Huck quite frequently and sometimes leaves him locked up in the cabin for as long as three days. Once when Pap returns from town, he is so drunk that he almost kills Huck. It is then that Huck decides that he has to find some way to escape — to avoid being killed.

The next day Huck discovers a canoe which he hides in the underbrush. When Pap catches some logs, he immediately leaves for town in order to sell them. Huck takes out a saw that he had hid, finishes sawing a hole in the wall, and then loads his canoe with provisions. He then shoots a wild pig, smashes the door of the cabin and scatters the pig's blood all over the place. He pulls out some of his own hair and sticks it on the back of the bloody axe, thereby giving the impression that he has been murdered. He then goes to the canoe and waits until dark. After a nap, he heads across the river for Jackson's Island, barely escaping detection from Pap, who is returning home.

Commentary

We see that in Pap's mind, money and education are juxtaposed, and since Pap has neither, he doesn't want Huck to have either. His frantic activities show him as a person to be avoided and Huck now intentionally goes to school "to spite pap."

It is a bizarre situation which Twain is presenting here when a father has to kidnap his own son. The entire relationship between Huck and his pap is endowed with the most extreme behavior on the part of Pap, and since Huck associates his own father with the evils of civilization, then the brutality of Pap becomes vaguely correlated in his mind with the brutality of civilization.

This father-son relationship stands as a contrast later on when Jim says that he will "steal" his own daughter if he can't free her in any other way. But Jim's comments are the result of his love and concern for his daughter. By this broad sweeping contrast between Huck and Pap and between Jim and his daughter, Twain is making a broad comment on the nature of parental love which cuts through the stereotyped view that *naturally* a white father would care more for his child than would a black father.

Huck's adaptability is again emphasized in this chapter. Earlier, in Chapter IV, Huck had reached a point where he "was getting sort of used to the widow's ways, too, and they warn't so raspy on me." Then after two months of living with Pap in the wilderness, he became so adjusted that he "didn't see how I'd ever got to like it so well at the widow's...." Thus, one of Huck's major attributes is his ability to adapt to any situation and to live in a variety of different surroundings, including the comfort of the raft later on.

In Chapter VI, Huck definitely seems to prefer the freedom of the wilderness to the restrictions of society. However, his freedom is modified by the presence of Pap, and the very safety of his life is often threatened by Pap's actions. Huck is mature enough to recognize the danger and only when he becomes convinced that Pap represents an immediate threat to his life does he decide upon the necessity of an escape.

Furthermore, Pap's actions toward him are a violation of Huck's belief that everyone should be kind to everyone else. His concept of freedom, then, is modified only when he feels that his life is endangered and that Pap does not "feel right and kind toward . . . others," which Huck uses as a basis for his own actions. The freedom is also modified by Huck's feelings of loneliness and isolation, particularly when Pap leaves him locked up.

Pap's drunken tirade against the "prowling, thieving, infernal, white-shirted free niger. . . ." fully illustrates a basic concept about prejudice. The lower and the more incompetent the dregs of humanity are, the oftener they preach subservience so as to protect their own inadequacies.

The final actions in Chapter VI convince Huck of the necessity of putting his escape plan into action immediately. Throughout his plans to escape, he is more concerned for his life than he is about anything else. He makes no attempt to inform people that he is alive so that his six thousand dollars will be protected — in fact, he knows that even if he were to try secretly to protect it that his pap might find out. Huck prefers simply to disappear and begin a new life, especially since, as we have seen, material comforts connected with great wealth are not important to Huck.

Huck's plan for escape is one of simple common sense combined with shrewdness and imagination. Ironically, he wishes that Tom Sawyer were there to give the plan the "fancy touches," but the reader knows that Huck is totally wrong. If Tom were there, the entire plan would probably fail or would soon be exposed as a trick even if Huck escaped. Tom's plans always carry a large dose of romantic falseness and absurdity. Thus, ultimately, Huck's plan here, based upon common sense, necessity, and shrewd judgment contrasts to Tom's pretentious and ridiculous plans at the Phelps' plantation. Again this is Twain's insistence that common sense and natural actions are to be valued above romantic pretensions. The plans also illustrate clearly that Huck will be able to take care of himself in the *larger* world, and suggests, by contrast, that Tom Sawyer, left to his own artificial ingenuity, would soon perish.

CHAPTERS VIII AND IX

Summary

The next day, Huck knows that his plan was a success when he sees a ferryboat filled with the important people of the town searching for his body. A cannon which is fired to make the body come to the surface almost kills Huck, and a loaf of bread which is supposed to lead them to the body floats to Huck's hiding place and he eats it for his breakfast.

After they leave, Huck is left alone on the island for three days and nights and begins to get lonesome. On the third day, he discovers the remains of a camp fire. Huck is frightened and paddles over to the Illinois shore, but fearing discovery from some travelers, he returns and keeps watch over the place where he discovered the ashes. Soon, Miss Watson's Jim appears and

Huck is awfully glad to see him. Thinking Huck is dead, Jim is frightened by Huck's "ghost." Huck tells him that he isn't dead, and they talk about their adventures. Jim confesses to Huck that he has run away because Miss Watson was about to sell him down south. Huck promises not to tell on Jim, even though "people would call me a low down Ablitionist and despise me for keeping mum. . . ."

During the next few days, Jim and Huck move their supplies to a cavern at the top of the hill on Jackson's Island. They spend their days collecting various things on the river that have floated loose because of the rising river water. Among the choice possessions they find is a large raft twelve feet wide and fifteen or sixteen feet long.

One night, they see a two-story frame house float by. They catch up with it and climb aboard to see if they can find any useful articles. While there, they discover a dead man who had been shot in the back. Jim quickly throws some rags over the corpse so that Huck won't have to see this gruesome sight. They load their canoe with all the worthwhile stuff in the cabin and head back to Jackson's Island.

Commentary

With Chapter VIII, Twain introduces another of his larger themes, that of death and rebirth. In terms of the entire novel, Huck symbolically dies in this chapter to be born again with a new set of values. The rebirth begins immediately when Huck encounters Jim, the runaway slave. Having died to the society from which he is escaping, Huck has spent three days in total isolation and loneliness—"by-and-by it got sort of lonesome." Thus, the encounter with Jim represents Huck's need for some sort of human companionship.

The need for human contact is pitted against Huck's past values as Jim confesses that he has run off. Huck knows that people (society) would "call me a low down Ablitionist and despise me for keeping mum," but he decides to keep his word to Jim in spite of the dictates of society. Had Huck not escaped from society, from Pap, and possibly death at the hands of Pap, then Huck's reaction to Jim's escape might have been different. This acceptance of Jim foreshadows Huck's later set of values when he totally defies society for the sake of his friendship with Jim.

Huck's rebirth is, therefore, first seen in his decision to help Jim and is set against the background of the society from which he is escaping. The irony is that when Huck was kidnapped by his father, the Widow Douglas made a nominal attempt to rescue Huck, but not until the boy is thought to be dead is there a full scale effort to rescue his body. Twain's satire on American values is obvious; society is more concerned about a dead body than it is in the welfare of living people. And, as we find out in Chapter XI, there is a three-hundred-dollar reward for the capture of Jim, but only two hundred dollars are offered for the capture of Huck's murderer.

These two chapters also continue Twain's contrast between the natural, or practical, sense of Huck set against superstitions of varying sorts. First, there are the actions of the seemingly educated people of town—Judge Thatcher, Tom Sawyer, Aunt Polly, Sid, the captain, etc.—who superstitiously load up bread with quicksilver which, ironically, feeds Huck and who shoot cannons over the water which, ironically, almost kills Huck.

The superstitions receive greater credence since they are seen against Huck's practical and natural actions of hiding his canoe, concealing his traps, preparing a camp under cover, and in escaping detection. It is also very natural and practical the way he is able to discover whose campfire he stumbles across. Then, Huck's first appearance causes Jim to think that he has seen a real ghost.

The practical, or natural, sense and superstitions are brought together in Jim's predictions. In almost all of Jim's superstitious utterings, there is embedded very practical, common sense knowledge. For example, Jim watches the actions of the birds and predicts the weather, which is good frontier practicality. Man can often predict certain natural events by observing the actions of the animals. Furthermore, in Jim's predictions about wealth, he leaves so much leeway that there is a practical sense about his views in that they could come true in many different ways. Jim also points out that no one needs to know any good luck signs because no one wants to prevent good luck.

Jim and Huck do share one trait in common — both are literal minded. Like Huck, who tried to pray for fish hooks, Jim thinks that if he gives money away he will "git his money back a hund'd times." Also, he considers himself rich now that he owns himself.

In Chapter VIII, Jim introduces his plan to escape by getting to the Illinois side of the river and later going up the Ohio River to free territory. Illinois, which was just across the river from slave territory, was historically not sympathetic to runaway slaves, and often they were returned by professional bounty hunters. Therefore, the more practical plan would be to go up the Ohio River to a state sympathetic to freeing the slave.

In Chapter IX, Jim and Huck establish a rather good place to live, and this serenity will not be interrupted until Huck discovers the plan of the townsmen to come looking on Jackson's Island for the runaway slave. From their base they are able to capture various items which float down the river. The frame house with the dead body in it attests to the fact that Twain had already planned on the death of Pap at this stage in the novel, but he will not reveal this fact until the last chapter of the novel.

CHAPTERS X AND XI

Summary

After breakfast, Huck wants to talk about the dead man, but Jim refuses to do so, saying that it might bring them bad luck. The bad luck comes in terms of a practical joke which Huck plays on Jim. He kills a rattlesnake and curls it up at the foot of Jim's bed, thinking it will be fun to watch Jim's reaction when he sees it. But the rattlesnake's mate crawls up around the dead one and when Jim returns, the mate bites him. Huck realizes that it happens because he was "such a fool as to not remember that wherever you leave a dead snake its mate always comes there and curls around it." Huck quickly throws the two snakes away before Jim can discover what happened. Jim is sick for four days and nights before he recovers. After a few days, Huck becomes restless and wants to know what is going on in town. Jim advises him to dress up like a girl in some of the clothes that they salvaged from the floating house. He heads out for the shore and, in town, he finds a house of a woman who is a newcomer. He decides to talk with this woman, trying hard to remember that he is a girl.

Huck identifies himself as Sarah Williams and, as he talks with the lady, he learns of the gossip and rumors connected with the separate disappearances of Huck and Jim. Although the lady has lived in the town only two weeks, she is already well informed in regard to the different theories of the supposed murder of Huck and the disappearance of Jim. The two murder suspects are Jim and Pap. Some people think that Pap did it in order to get Huck's money without bothering with a lawsuit. Others think that Jim did it, since he ran away the same night that Huck disappeared. There is a three-hundred dollar reward offered for Jim and a two-hundred dollar reward for Pap.

When Huck hears the lady say that she has seen smoke on Jackson's Island and that her husband is going over to see if he could capture Jim, Huck becomes so anxious that he forgets that he is a girl. Using several basic tests, the lady soon discovers that Huck is a boy. Huck then admits that he is in disguise and invents another story about his escape from a hard master and his flight to Goshen. He is promptly informed, however, that this is not Goshen; it is St. Petersburg. He convinces her that someone has played a trick on him and leaves as soon as possible.

After Huck leaves, he goes as quickly as possible back to Jackson's Island, starts a fire in the old camp site, then goes to find Jim. When he comes upon Jim, he tells him to get ready quickly because "They're after us!" Since their raft is already loaded, it takes only a few minutes to leave, and they glide along the shady side of the island until they have passed the foot of the island.

Commentary

Chapter X presents the climax of the theme of superstition when Jim is bitten by the rattlesnake. This is the first time that Huck has done something which shows that he is not using common sense. He knows that the mate to a dead snake always comes and curls around the dead one, and yet he left the dead snake there anyway. This lapse from common sense causes Jim to get bitten.

On another level, the episode with the snake bite shows Huck performing a Tom Sawyer-type of trick. Huck will pull only one more trick on Jim and then will develop into a more mature person. His deep regret at pulling this trick on Jim indicates the beginning of a deep relationship. We can assume that Tom Sawyer would not have the deep regret that Huck does.

Ultimately, whenever something bad happens later in the novel, Jim will blame it on the bad luck caused by the rattlesnake, which then involves Huck more intricately because the bad luck was caused by Huck himself. The superstition motif is brought to a climax because the remedies which Jim uses have the therapeutic effect of making Jim drunk enough so that he won't feel the pain.

The superstition theme is used at the beginning of the chapter so that Jim will not have to tell Huck that he saw Pap dead in the floating cabin. Jim's refusal to talk about the death carries several implications. First, the news is not revealed until the last page of the novel, thus attesting to the fact that Twain had planned ahead to the ending of his novel. Second, Jim's refusal might be selfish in that if Pap is dead, one more obstacle is removed from Huck's need to flee society, thus leaving Jim stranded in his flight. But, more important, as we later discover,

Jim feels so devoted to his own children that he assumes that this would be a terrible tragedy for Huck and therefore wants to spare Huck any feelings of grief. The implied comparison between Jim's love for his family and the brutality in Pap's relation to Huck will be later developed and will be one of the values by which Huck learns of Jim's humanity and love for others.

At the end of Chapter X, Huck is preparing to make his first journey to shore. The need to know whether Jim's escape was successful prompts the trip ashore and becomes the first of many subsequent adventures which pit the life on the raft against the life of society on the shore. Chapter XI also represents the end of the idyllic existence that Jim and Huck have been enjoying on the island.

Huck's trip ashore dressed as a girl is one of the classic excerpts from the novel and has often appeared separately. Thematically, this is another identity for Huck, and it is also the beginning of many different types of identities he will assume throughout their long journey.

Also introduced in this chapter is Huck's ability to invent stories. While Huck is fantastic, shrewd, and imaginative in creating a believable story which will conceal his real identity, he is also unable to remember the story which he tells and often has to resort to another ruse or shrewd trick in order to find out what he said earlier. As he says in a later chapter (XXXII), he seldom has a particular plan in mind, but, instead, he goes along "trusting to Providence to put the right words in my mouth when the time come." In other words, Huck relies upon his native ability, whereas Tom Sawyer has to have some ridiculous or fantastic plan.

While Huck is able to create believable stories, he is unable to fool the shrewd country woman. The tricks which she uses to reveal his identity as a boy have become classic. But while she traps Huck in his disguise, he is able to construct another story which gets him out of difficulty.

At the end of Chapter XI, Huck, having discovered that some men are going to Jackson's Island to look for Jim, returns as quickly as possible to the island and tells Jim: "Git up and hump yourself, Jim! There ain't a minute to lose. They're after us!" However they are *not* after *them*, only Jim. But by this time Huck has so completely identified with Jim and Jim's plight that he accepts Jim's struggle as his own. This, then, leads to his later acceptance of Jim as superior to the values of a society which would enslave him.

Chapter XI ends the first part of the novel and, with the next chapter, we enter into the second section, the experiences along the Mississippi River.

CHAPTERS XII AND XIII

Summary

It is almost one o'clock before they get below the island. At daybreak they tie the raft to a tow-head on the Illinois side which is covered with trees and bushes so that they are protected from sight. Here they can watch the steamboats go by. Huck tells Jim about the conversation with the lady in the cabin and how he built the fire to make the men stay there to catch Jim when he returned.

Jim builds a tent in the middle of the raft for protection from the weather. He and Huck also make an extra steering oar for emergencies. For five nights they travel down the river, lying on their backs and looking at the stars. Every night, Huck slips ashore for provisions. Five nights below St. Louis, they encounter a big storm and they board a wrecked steamboat, even though Jim tries to dissuade Huck from boarding it.

Once on the steamboat, they see a light down the "texas-hall" and overhear a conversation between two robbers, Jake Packard and Bill, who are about to murder an accomplice, Jim Turner, because he threatened to inform on them. At this point, Huck has to crawl into a stateroom on the upper side to keep from being detected. The thieves accidentally follow him into the room but Huck is able to hide from them. Packard argues that instead of murdering Turner they should take their boat ashore and leave Jim Turner on the wreck which will break up in two hours and wash down the river. Huck goes back to tell Jim and to set the robbers' boat adrift so that the men cannot get away. At this point, Jim reveals that the raft has broken loose in the storm, and they are also stranded.

Huck and Jim look for and find the boat (skiff) that the robbers arrived in. Just as they are about to board the skiff, Packard and Bill appear, arguing about the money which they left in Jim Turner's pocket. They decide to go back and get it. Huck and Jim then jump into the boat, cut the rope and escape, leaving all three cutthroats stranded on the foundering boat.

Before they are able to notify anyone about the wrecked boat, a summer storm comes up and a flash of lightning reveals their raft floating ahead of them. They recapture it, and Jim guides the raft while Huck follows in the skiff until they see the lights of a village on a hillside. Huck startles the sleeping watchman of a ferryboat and relates one of his stories designed to force the watchman to rescue the people on the wrecked boat. Artfully giving the impression that the niece of the richest man in town is on the boat, Huck influences the watchmen to rescue the cutthroats.

In a few minutes, the wreck comes floating along. It is so deep in the water that Huck knows that no one could still be alive, but he paddles around it and hollers. After hearing no sound, Huck gives up and goes to catch up with Jim. By now, it is daylight and they pull to shore and sleep "like dead people."

Commentary

Chapter XII begins the second major part of the novel and covers the various adventures down the Mississippi River until Jim is sold back into slavery. This chapter begins the odyssey down the river, which immediately takes upon a mythic quality as Huck notes the contentment found by escaping from society: "It was kind of solemn, drifting down the big still river, laying on our backs looking up at the stars. . . ."

The first significant adventure involves the wreck of the *Walter Scott* which Jim and Huck discover one night. The name of the wreck is one of Twain's subtle uses of satire since he apparently thought Walter Scott's novels, and any romantic novels, were something of a wreck which foundered when they tried to sail.

With this adventure and others like it, Huck constantly wishes that Tom Sawyer were along because this is much closer to life than were the Sunday School picnic raids which Tom used to organize. But Huck doesn't fully realize the inherent danger he is in when he embarks upon this adventure.

The purpose of boarding the vessel is to see if they can rescue anything of value from the wreck. Discovering the cutthroats and murderers on board, Huck is almost trapped since the raft has floated away, but is saved only by the greed of the men who return to get Jim Turner's "loot" before leaving him to his destiny.

Huck's first thought after escaping is to save Jim Turner (a murderer) from being murdered by the other two cutthroats, showing again Huck's sympathy for human beings. Even after he escapes, he conceives of the clever plan of sending the man with the ferry in order to try and save all three of the cutthroats from death. His sympathy with even the worse dregs of society allows Huck to respond to all classes of people and prepares us for his total acceptance of Jim.

Having attempted to save them, Huck ironically and erroneously thinks that the Widow Douglas would be proud of him for protecting the lives of these cutthroats because "helping . . . rapscallions and dead beats is the kind the widow and good people takes the most interest in."

Chapter XIII also shows again Huck's ingenuity in creating a story which serves his purpose. He hears the old ferryman

34

speak jealously of the wealth of someone named Hornback and then Huck creates a story about Hornback's niece being trapped on the sinking boat—a story which immediately causes the ferryman to attempt a rescue mission.

CHAPTER XIV

Summary

When Huck and Jim awaken, they examine the loot which the robbers took from the wreck and find all sorts of valuable things, along with many books which Huck reads to Jim. The books contain tales of kings and dukes and earls and their many adventures in life. The only figure familiar to Jim is "King Sollermum," who was not a good person, in Jim's opinion, because King Solomon would have divided a child into two parts. Huck tries to explain the story of King Solomon to Jim, but Jim will not change his opinion. Furthermore, the entire concept of anyone speaking a language different from English is also astonishing to Jim who thinks that if a Frenchman is a man then he should speak like a man.

Commentary

Chapter XIV functions as a kind of interlude in which Huck and Jim enjoy some of the rewards (such as the cigars) which they got from the wrecked *Walter Scott*. If later in the novel, Huck seems to possess too much knowledge of history and other matters for a person of about fourteen years, we must remember that they rescue "lots of books" from the wreck and that Huck spends much of his leisure time reading them to himself and Jim. Since we have already seen Huck's practical and shrewd knowledge in operation, there is no reason to conclude that he cannot equally master "book" knowledge.

Furthermore, his reading about history and the discussion of the "dolphin" (dauphin) prepares us for the appearance and story of the "king" in Chapter XIX. Historically, there were persistent rumors, known even on the frontier, that the Dauphin, Louis

Charles (born 1785) had escaped execution and had fled to the new world. At the time of the novel, then, he would be about fifty-five years old, instead of seventy, which is the age of the "king."

This chapter also obliquely presents some more of Twain's satire against religion. For a person like Jim, who is in bondage or slavery, the stories of Christianity and of the Bible have little meaning to him and are often incomprehensible. As noted earlier, the concept of forcing slaves (property) to become practicing Christians is a violation of the concept of Christianity.

CHAPTERS XV AND XVI

Summary

In three more nights, Huck and Jim expect to reach Cairo, where they will sell the raft and catch a steamboat up the Ohio River. On the second night, however, there is so much fog that Huck takes the canoe and tries to find a place for them to tie up. Because of the swift current, the raft floats by and Huck cannot find Jim and the raft. He searches until he is exhausted and then falls asleep.

When he awakens, he sees the raft close by, filled with leaves and all sorts of trash, and Jim is asleep from worry and exhaustion. Huck slips onto the raft and when Jim finally wakes up, Huck tries to make him think that they have never been separated and that Jim dreamed everything that happened to them. When he has Jim almost convinced that it was all a dream, he asks Jim to interpret the dream — which Jim does; next, Huck asks him to interpret all the trash and branches on the raft. Then Jim realizes the truth and tells Huck that trash is "people . . . dat puts dirt on de head er dey fren's en makes 'em ashamed." Huck apologizes to Jim and vows to himself that he will never play a trick on Jim again.

Jim knows that they must be close to Cairo and therefore close to freedom, and he begins to talk about his freedom in a jubilant manner. Suddenly Huck's conscience begins to trouble him because he knows that he is helping someone else's property to escape. But then Jim says that if the owner of his children will not sell Jim his children, then he will get an abolitionist to help steal them. This is almost more than Huck can stand, and he knows suddenly that he is doing an awful thing in helping Jim to escape, and he resolves to slip ashore and tell. As he takes a canoe to go tell, Jim calls out that he will never forget what a good friend Huck has been to him.

When Huck meets some men looking for some runaway slaves, he cannot bring himself to betray Jim. Instead, he creates a story about his father on the raft having smallpox, and the men become frightened and give Huck money with instructions that he should never let it be known that his father has smallpox when he is seeking help. After the men leave, Huck feels again that he has done wrong, but it is too much bother to do right.

Later, Huck and Jim try to find out if they have passed Cairo, and when they see the clear water of the Ohio, they know that they have already passed the town. They go to the canoe so as to paddle back upstream, but the canoe has disappeared. As they continue downstream, a steamboat approaches them and, before they can get out of its way, the boat smashes directly into the raft. Jim goes overboard on one side and Huck on the other. Huck stays underwater until the thirty-foot wheel has passed over him. Soon the boat is churning along upstream again, but Huck cannot find Jim. He goes ashore alone, where he finds dogs barking in front of a large house.

Commentary

In these two chapters, Twain reached a crucial point in his narrative which was difficult to resolve. Somewhere along this point (probably toward the end of Chapter XVI), Twain put the manuscript aside and did not begin writing on it again for about two years.

After having Jim and Huck pass Cairo and the mouth of the Ohio River, Twain's original plan for Jim to escape up the Ohio

River must have been abandoned; but if this is so, it undercuts the larger theme of Jim's quest for freedom because the farther down the Mississippi they travel, the deeper they travel into slave territory. But, apparently, Twain was more concerned with the type of freedom represented by Huck and Jim on the raft, as contrasted to the imprisonment, the cruelty, and inhumanity represented by Huck's many encounters on the land.

In Chapter XV, when Jim and Huck get separated by the currents, Huck's loneliness is emphasized so as to stress the importance of his and Jim's relationship. Huck, however, still has some of his youthfulness about him and decides to fool Jim. The trick he plays on Jim is the last juvenile thing that Huck does until Tom Sawyer appears in the final part of the novel.

When Huck plays this trick on Jim, he fails to recognize the fullness of Jim's devotion to him. After Jim's classic definition of what is "trash," Huck understands the fullness of Jim's humanity and vows to play no more tricks on him. This recognition and Huck's resolve to "humble myself to a nigger" attest to his maturing and to his accepting the innate value of the human being. Furthermore, one of Huck's basic attributes is that he treats everyone kindly. Throughout the novel, he cannot stand the idea of even scoundrels having something mean done to them.

In Chapter XVI, after Huck's changing view of Jim, he has to pit his own values against those of society and those of his own conscience. When Huck hears that Jim is jubilant at the thought of escape, and also that Jim plans to steal, if necessary, his own children out of slavery, he is horrified at such audacity and shocked at his own part in such an "immoral" undertaking.

Huck's shock and his troubled conscience must be viewed historically in terms of his going against church, society, and state as he helps the runaway slave. Huck is not old enough or experienced enough to recognize the importance of his own values and the falseness of those of society. Thus, his conflict here is a sincere one in which he is deeply troubled over his actions.

The irony reaches cosmic proportions when a man has to try to buy his children and, if he can't buy them, he must steal them – "children that belonged to a man I didn't even know, a man that hadn't ever done me no harm." Here the lesser sin of "stealing" is placed against the greater sin of enslaving a race. The horror of this situation causes Huck to decide to reveal Jim's presence – an act which, according to society, would elevate Huck's moral position.

The thought of telling on Jim is juxtaposed to the encounter with the bounty hunters who are out to capture some runaway slaves. At the crucial moment, Huck cannot bring himself to inform on Jim, thus showing that his innate sense of right exceeds that of society.

The larger irony of the situation lies in Huck's thinking that he is committing a great sin by protecting Jim – while at the same time we see the slave hunters who are hunting down humans but will not help a theoretically sick man. Huck's ingenuity is seen both in the story which he tells the men and, more directly, in his knowledge that the men, being selfish and narrow, will not help him. This illustrates that Huck has more than the ingenuity to create a story – that he has a profound knowledge of human nature which allows him to create stories which play upon the selfishness and pettiness of the slave hunters.

The men think they remove their moral obligation by giving Huck some money. Thus, we have a contrast between their refusal to commit themselves to helping another human being and Huck's commitment to protect Jim. As the men leave to track down the slaves, Huck is troubled in his conscience, but we must assume that the men are not bothered by their duplicity and selfishness as they go back to hunting slaves and feeling that they have discharged their responsibilities by giving a sum of money. Few scenes in the novel capture the essential inhumanity of society as well as does this powerful scene.

At the end of Chapter XVI, both Huck and Jim recognize by the clear water in the Mississippi that they have passed the mouth of the Ohio River. Again, Jim blames this piece of bad luck on the rattlesnake.

Twain has the canoe lost in this chapter so that they can't go back and paddle up the Ohio River. Realistically, then, they must wait until they can find a canoe so as to return to the mouth of the river. This is the excuse for continuing down the Mississippi River — a river which Twain was familiar with — rather than going up the Ohio — a river which Twain did not know. The destruction of the raft at the end of the chapter is another indication that Twain was puzzled over how to continue his story, and it is at this point that critics have projected that Twain laid aside his manuscript for two years.

CHAPTERS XVII AND XVIII

Summary

At the house, Huck is forced to identify himself. He tells the man confronting him that he is George Jackson and that he fell overboard from a passing steamboat. He invents another fantastic story which the people believe. This house belongs to a wealthy landowner, whose youngest child is Buck, about Huck's age. The two boys share a bedroom together and soon become good friends.

The house is furnished in a manner that impresses Huck, but of special interest to him are the crayon drawings made by Emmeline Grangerford, who died when she was fourteen. Most of the drawings are of rather morbid subjects. Her attempts at poetry about dead people are also rated high by her relatives and by Huck. On the whole, Huck is very content to be here since there is so much good food.

While living with the Grangerfords, Huck is impressed by their manners and mode of living. Every member of the family has a Negro servant, including Huck. The only other aristocratic family is named Shepherdson and, one day while Huck and Buck are walking, Buck jumps behind a bush and shoots at young

Harney Shepherdson. Huck is confused, and Buck explains that the two families are having a feud. Since Huck has never heard of a feud, Buck has to explain that it is a type of quarrel in which everyone on one side wants to kill everyone on the other side until "by and by everybody's killed off, and there ain't no more feud." This particular feud has been going on for thirty years and everyone has forgotten how it started.

One day when Huck is delivering a message for Miss Sophia Grangerford, his servant takes him down to the river. There he discovers Jim in hiding. Jim has been collecting material and preparing the raft for the day when he and Huck can continue their journey.

With the knowledge that Miss Sophia has run off with Harney Shepherdson, the feud breaks out with more intensity. So many Grangerfords and Shepherdsons are killed that Huck is sorry that he ever came on shore. He escapes as quickly as possible, rejoins Jim, and they continue their journey down the river.

Commentary

These two chapters dealing with the Grangerford and Shepherdson feud allow Twain to satirize many aspects of American culture. In general, Twain is against such feuds, which were still known to exist in parts of the country. Twain reveals the senseless brutality and the needless manslaughter involved in such an arbitrary concept of honor. For Twain, such a feud goes counter to common sense and anything that violated common sense was abhorrent to Twain.

The feud itself has overtones of a Romeo and Juliet story placed in the Kentucky wilderness. It has gone on so long that the people do not even know why they are fighting; yet, embedded in the bloody feud are many artificial concepts of honor and behavior. For example, Mr. Grangerford tells Buck that he shouldn't shoot from behind a bush but should step out in the road to kill a Shepherdson.

Huck's reaction to this needless slaughter is finally one of sickness and revulsion for such a waste of human life. Huck's practicality here, then, is important because it allows him to see through the superficial concepts which keep the feud alive and to evaluate it according to his common sense.

In terms of the larger thematic patterns, we see Huck again using his shrewdness on shore as he creates yet another new identity for himself. When he forgets his name, he has to be shrewd enough to conceive a plan whereby Buck Grangerford will spell his name. Huck has such an understanding of people that he easily gulls a boy the same age, one who loves to show off his knowledge of spelling, into spelling Huck's assumed name. Thus Huck is able to rediscover his new identity.

Huck's literal mindedness is emphasized again in this section as he fails to catch the point of the joke about Moses and the candle. This same literal minded quality will allow him to evaluate the impractical waste of human life in the feud. This same quality also allows Huck to report directly about other aspects of the Grangerford life, and his direct reporting without evaluating underscores Twain's satire.

For example, Twain's satire against, and parody of, the type of sentimental poetry written during his day is seen in Huck's "appreciation" of Emmeline Grangerford's sickening verse. That Huck is impressed by this poetry ("If Emmeline Grangerford could make poetry like that before she was fourteen, there ain't no telling what she could a done by-and-by.") is part of Twain's technique of using Huck as a realistic reporter rather than one who evaluates for us. Yet, even Huck finally becomes "soured on her a little" because of her predilection for death and morbidity. (Historically, Twain is satirizing specifically the poetry of Julia A. Moore who called herself "the Sweet Singer of Michigan"; Twain called her the "Queen and Empress of the Hogwash Guild.")

Huck's description of the Grangerford house emphasizes all the taudry, cheap objects which decorate the house. All of this satire is against those who have a predilection for morbid works of art, sentimental poetry, and bad taste in almost everything.

As long as Huck hears about the feud in vague terms, he is not terribly concerned about it. But once he becomes involved and observes the brutality of Buck's death, his horror surpasses direct expression. It is only by contrast with the return to the river that Huck can express his disapproval of such senseless brutality: "It made me so sick I most fell out of the tree. I ain't agoing to tell *all* that happened—it would make me sick again if I was to do that. I wished I hadn't ever come ashore that night. . . ." The contrast between the horror of events on shore and the freedom of the raft is a comment upon the inhumanity of society in general.

Back on the raft, Huck feels "free and safe once more." Part of the irony is that in contrast to the small, confined raft, "other places do feel so cramped up and smothery, but a raft don't. You feel mighty free and easy and comfortable on a raft." By this oblique statement, Huck arrives at a metaphysical evaluation of the contrast between the idyllic life of peace and brotherhood of himself and Jim as opposed to the inhumanity of the feud and the values of society.

CHAPTERS XIX AND XX

Summary

Two or three days and nights slide by as they travel by night and hide by day. One morning about daybreak, Huck finds a canoe, crosses to the main shore, and paddles up a creek looking for berries. Suddenly he hears two men being pursued by dogs and other men are following the dogs. When the pursued men beg Huck to save them, he quickly tells them the best way to throw the dogs off their scent.

One man is seventy and bald; the other is about thirty. They are not acquainted but both were run out of the town because of their efforts to defraud the citizens by cheating, quackery, and other fraudulent schemes. Once on the raft, the youngest claims to be the rightful Duke of Bridgewater. After Huck and Jim hear his sad story, they begin to treat him with respect. The older man then tells them that he is the lost Dauphin of France. Huck, however, is not deceived and knows that the two are nothing more than "humbugs and frauds."

They question Huck about the presence of Jim on the raft and are temporarily satisfied when Huck assures them that a runaway slave would never run south. Huck then invents another fantastic story to protect both Jim and himself.

The two frauds soon appropriate both beds in the wigwam, leaving Jim and Huck out in the rain. By this time, even Jim doesn't want any more kings and dukes to appear. The two frauds pool their resources and decide to rehearse a Shakespearian presentation of *Romeo and Juliet,* letting the seventy-year-old king play the part of Juliet. When the raft stops for provisions near a small town, the king wanders into a camp meeting where he pretends to be a reformed pirate in need of money to go back and reform the other pirates. By this ruse, he is able to collect eighty-seven dollars and seventy cents.

Meanwhile, the duke goes to a printing office where he cheats the owner out of nine dollars and, at the same time, prints a handbill describing Jim as a runaway slave from forty miles below New Orleans. If anyone questions them, they will simply say that they are returning Jim for the reward.

Commentary

By this time in the novel, all thought of returning to Cairo and going up the Ohio River is set aside. Now Twain emphasizes the peaceful, calm, and quiet qualities of the river which will function as a contrast to the difficulty Huck and Jim have with the duke and king later on.

The appearance of two men being pursued immediately evokes sympathy from Huck, and he is anxious to help. He is also shrewd enough to give them the best method of covering up their escape.

The traveling confidence man, or fraud, is common to many types of frontier literature, but Twain, by individualizing these two "types," makes them into fully realized characters. These people have to possess a certain degree of cleverness in order to dupe people so successfully. Their success is often based upon their ability to analyze the society which they are going to defraud and thus take advantage of it because that society, through its ignorance, allows itself to be defrauded.

The stories of the king (Dauphin) and the duke have been prepared for by Huck's earlier reading in history. After the duke receives special treatment because of his impressive story, the king tells an even bigger lie in order to receive preferential treatment. At first, we are led to believe that Huck believes these stories, but by the end of the chapter, his shrewdness surpasses his literal mindedness. He sees through their ruse: "It didn't take me long to make up my mind that these liars warn't no kings nor dukes, at all, but just low-down humbugs and frauds."

It is necessary for Huck to have this insight since it allows him to realize that they would sell Jim at the first opportune moment. Thus he temporarily protects Jim with another shrewd story, one which both the king and duke seem to believe. Therefore, Huck's shrewdness exceeds both the king's and duke's since he sees through their facade and is able to make his own story credible. Huck's insight also suggests his knowledge of human nature, a knowledge which has the practical purpose of protecting both himself and Jim.

The absurdity of the plan to present *Romeo and Juliet* is another comment upon the stupidity of their audience. Throughout these scenes, Twain's point is that the gullibility of the average person allows such rogues to function. However, historically speaking, the parts of women were still played by young boys so that the audience would not expect a real lady; nevertheless, Juliet was *never* played by a seventy-year-old, bald-headed man;

only the most credulous audience would accept such an absurdity.

A stock situation in frontier humor is a rogue who goes to a revival meeting, confesses to any type of sin, pretends to reform, takes up a collection, and then flees with the money. (For example, see Johnson J. Hooper's "Simon Suggs Attends a Camp-Meeting.") Twain, however, takes this basic situation and turns it into sophisticated art. The basis of the humor is again the gullibility of the audience and also the king's knowledge that the audience takes a vicarious delight in hearing about evil. The more evil a person, the more delightful is his reform. Since the audience is so gullible, Huck does not take a moral stand, the emphasis again being that such an audience deserves to be defrauded.

The episode with the handbill suggests something of the cleverness and shrewdness of the duke. We realize that both of these rogues are clever enough to live by their wits. By the end of the chapter, however, even Jim has recognized that they are scoundrels and hopes that he and Huck don't meet any more "kings" and "dukes" on their trip.

CHAPTERS XXI, XXII, AND XXIII

Summary

The king and the duke begin to rehearse for the Shakespearean production which they will present in some town along the river. When they arrive in a small Arkansas town, there is already a circus there. The duke distributes his advertisements of the show throughout the town.

While Huck is lounging around the town, a person named Boggs comes in from the country "for his little old monthly drunk." Everybody laughs at him as he proclaims drunkenly that he is there to "kill old Colonel Sherburn." While the townspeople are assuring Huck that Boggs is harmless, they are also sending for Boggs' daughter to take care of him. However, before she arrives, Boggs continues to insult Colonel Sherburn, who appears with a gun and shoots Boggs down in cold blood just as the daughter arrives.

Led by a man named Buck Harkness, a mob gathers, gets drunk, and then goes to Colonel Sherburn's house to lynch the murderer. The colonel calls them cowards and taunts them by saying that if any lynching is to be done, it will be done in the dark with a *man*, not half a man, as a leader. At the end of Colonel Sherburn's speech, the crowd "broke all apart and went tearing off every which way."

Huck, intent on seeing the circus, dives under the tent and marvels at the color and action of it all. Later, since only twelve people attend the Shakespearean performance, the duke and the king change to a performance where ladies and children are not admitted, thus assuring themselves of a good turnout.

The show is, of course, a fraud and a cheat, but those seeing it the first night do not admit being taken in and advise their neighbors to see the second performance. The third night, both audiences return, ready to tar and feather the king and the duke, but the two con men catch on to the audience's intent and escape to the raft after having cheated the town out of four hundred and sixty-five dollars.

Commentary

The Shakespearean production is in the best of the frontier humor tradition where bits and pieces of fractured Shakespeare were carelessly put together. The ability to do even this suggests something of their cleverness. In fact, the entire episode reveals them to be so clever that Huck recognizes how dangerous they are and knows that he must be extremely careful so as to protect Jim.

Basically, the circus in the town helps them put over their schemes. We should note that throughout the entire proceeding, Huck remains the observer and not a participant. In other words, he retains a moral neutrality which will change only in the Wilks episode. The importance of his moral neutrality is that the audience, being so gullible, deserves to be defrauded by these scoundrels.

After the Shakespearean program flops, the rogues conceive of the plan to attract an audience by presenting a show where "Ladies and Children" are not admitted, knowing that man's propensity for the vulgar will draw a large audience. The show, "The King's Camelopard or The Royal Nonesuch," is based upon vulgar, obscene, and coarse humor, essentially degrading in its nature, and the large crowd that gathers is Twain's method of saying that man is base and depraved.

The ultimate cleverness of the rogues is illustrated in the fact that they know that the town plans to punish them, but they are always one step ahead of the townspeople. The amount of money, $465.00, becomes important in the next episode when they add most of that amount to the Wilks hoard.

These chapters also show Twain's undisguised contempt for certain aspects of frontier life and, more important, his dislike for "the damned human race," the title of a later work by Twain. The description of the town in Chapter XXI and of the bums who hang about the street shows Twain's dislike for shiftless, worthless men who live in a place where there is mud in the streets, where the livestock run freely, and where houses are run down, etc.

His contempt for man is fully illustrated in the Sherburn-Boggs episode which was based on a real event. Twain's contempt for mob action, and mobs in general, recurs in other of his works. Twain does not condone Sherburn's shooting down Boggs in cold blood. His point, however, is that one powerful man is stronger than any mob. Sherburn's contempt for the townspeople is also Twain's contempt for "the damned human race": "The average man's a coward," Sherburn maintains and then proves his statement by his actions. Further proof is that the mob has to get drunk before it can attempt to act.

The circus episode in Chapter XXII again shows Huck's literal mindedness and his tendency to report things factually. The comedy of this situation depends entirely upon Huck's narrative point of view in that he thinks that the ringmaster—and not he—was the person most deceived.

Huck's description of kings and rulers is highly comic on an intellectual basis. Some critics have complained that the fourteen-year-old Huck could not possibly know this much about history, and their complaint carries some value. However, Huck did find "a lot of books" in the floating cabin and he has been reading from the books on their trip down the river. The intellectual comedy results from the utter and grand confusion of history with fiction and in the manner in which Huck juxtaposes historical persons, incidents, and events which are centuries apart with occurrences from fictional narratives. The general point of the satire is that all kings or rulers or politicians are "mighty ornery" and "you couldn't tell them [the king and the duke] from the real kind."

At the end of the chapter, Jim tells his story of how he treated his daughter, 'Lizabeth. The purpose of the story is to further humanize Jim and to make us sympathize with him. In contrast to the manner in which Huck's pap treated him, we see a deeper love and humanity in Jim's relationship with his daughter. Furthermore, it forces Huck into another important recognition: "I do believe he cared just as much for his people as white folks does for their'n. It don't seem natural, but I reckon it's so." This recognition is another step toward Huck's total acceptance of Jim as an equal human being.

CHAPTER XXIV

Summary

Back on the raft and safe from the mob, the duke dresses Jim as a sick Arab so that he will not have to remain tied up all day when the others want to leave him. Then they all dress up in some "store bought" clothes, and the king tells Huck to paddle toward a steamboat. On the way, they meet a young country fellow who mistakes the king for a Mr. Wilks from England, whose brother, Peter Wilks, has just died leaving his two brothers a fortune. The king inquires into various details about Peter Wilks' family, about his financial holdings, and about other people who live in the town.

The young man, who is going to South America, is free with his information, telling the king all sorts of things about the town and its people. Later, the king has Huck paddle him to another town and then sends Huck to fetch the duke. Since Peter Wilks had another brother who was deaf and dumb, the king instructs the duke to pretend to be deaf and dumb, and then the two hail a steamboat and get off at the town posing as Peter Wilks' brothers. When Huck understands their plans, he feels that "it was enough to make a body ashamed of the human race."

Commentary

Chapters XXIV through XXX deal with the Wilks episode. In general, the entire episode satirizes the absolute gullibility of the human race and becomes one of Twain's most damning comments on the subject. His point is that only through the sentimentalizing and the gullibility of the general public can such rogues function. He also depicts the degree to which man wants to be deceived for sentimental reasons rather than face brutal reality.

In the revival scene, Huck was merely amused at how people deceive themselves, but in this episode, Twain shows his contempt for the "damned human race" which is about to create a grave injustice by so willingly embracing the effusive rogues. Ultimately we too must criticize the townspeople—almost as much as we do the rogues.

In this scene, Huck shifts from being an amused observer to becoming morally involved in the events. Huck's comment at the end of Chapter XXIV, "Well, if ever I struck anything like it, I'm a nigger. It was enough to make a body ashamed of the

human race," indicates that Huck is learning to make moral
evaluations. Earlier, the people gypped by the rogues were not
worthy of Huck's concern. The Wilks girls, however, are honest,
grief-stricken people who are about to be exploited, thus remov-
ing the rogues' actions from the realm of simple fraud and sinking it to the level of immoral exploitation. Huck's commitment
here to a moral stand leads ultimately to his final commitment
to Jim.

Huck's expression, damning the actions of the king and the
duke, involves his saying "I'm a nigger." When he says this, he
apparently does not consider Jim's friendship. Huck, unfortunately, still views Negroes as "niggers" and, therefore, as sub-
human. Because he uses the phrase — "I'm a nigger" — to express
the impossible, we realize that he has not, and perhaps cannot,
divorce himself completely from the standards of society.

Furthermore, at the beginning of Chapter XXIV, the inhumanity of tying up Jim all day shows a basic lack of regard for
Jim's personal worth. Huck, being physically afraid of the rogues,
can do nothing about this situation.

In the beginning of the episode, the technique which the
king uses to pump the young boy of all the information he can get
is an excellent example of the ability of the rogue to capitalize
on any situation. Huck is so literal minded that he cannot understand the king's purpose; he is confused and, therefore, reports
the episode without any comment. Only when he understands
the king's purpose does he make his first moral comment upon
the immorality of the scheme.

CHAPTERS XXV AND XXVI

Summary

The king and the duke put on an impressive act beside the
coffin of Mr. Wilks and have most of the town sobbing in sympathy. Using the names acquired from their young informant to
prove acquaintance with the leading citizens of the town, the

duke and the king make their case so plausible that no questions are asked. The king does all the talking, while the duke poses as the deaf mute brother.

The hoax is successful for a while. The nieces of Peter Wilks show his will to the king. The dwelling house and three thousand dollars are bequeathed to the girls and the remainder of the wealth, a considerable amount, goes to the brothers of Mr. Wilks. When the impostors count the money in the cellar, it is four hundred and fifteen dollars short. They make up the deficit and, as a magnanimous gesture, present the money to the girls. All the townspeople are impressed except one. Dr. Robinson, a close friend of the late Peter Wilks, sees through the deception and tries to get the girls to listen to him. But the girls continue to trust their bogus uncles and even turn their money over to them for investment.

At breakfast the next morning, the hare-lip, Joanna, asks Huck so many questions that he almost gives away the secret. Her older sisters, however, make her quit heckling Huck. Since the girls are so nice to him, Huck's conscience begins to bother him and, that evening, he spies on the king and the duke as they hide the money in a mattress. Huck removes it to his bedroom and lies awake all night guarding it, intending to restore it to the Wilks girls as soon as possible.

Commentary

Twain is known to sometime laspe into bad taste; for example, the episode in Chapter XXIII about the King's Cameleopard was reportedly tamed down for publication. In this episode, the use of a "hare-lip" is in bad taste. Any comedy at the expense of physical deformity is always considered in bad taste.

Greed will function as the denouement of the king and the duke. The king's greed for everything will ultimately be the cause of their failure. Ironically, most of the money they defrauded the town of Bricksville out of is added to the Wilks money. First, their cleverness is illustrated by the fact that they needed to add enough money to make it $3000.00 since that is what it should be. Thus, ironically, the girls ultimately profit from the rogues' effort to cheat them out of their inheritance.

This chapter also shows what Twain meant by people acting as a herd. One sensible person, Dr. Robinson, is ignored by the crowd, which is completely taken in by the artifice of the king and the duke.

In Chapter XXVI, Huck thinks he is about to be trapped by the hare-lip and involves himself in a series of lies. His fear, however, is unwarranted since the hare-lip is only bantering with Huck because she knows Huck is the typical fourteen-year-old who likes to exaggerate. She never doubts the idea that he comes from England, only that he is exaggerating in some of his stories about England.

Of great significance in Chapter XXVI is Huck's commit-ment to help the Wilks girls. Earlier, as noted above, Huck's re-fusal to hinder the king and the duke was based upon the corruptness of society. As an outcast from society, Huck, in pro-tecting Jim, has already violated many rules of society. However, we have seen in many episodes that he instinctively responds to the individual and his needs. Since he admires and respects Mary Jane and since he knows that she is about to be cheated out of her inheritance, he is drawn morally into the episode and de-termines at great danger to himself to save their inheritance. Ironically, money, which is not terribly important to Huck, be-comes a motivating factor in his decision to help the ladies since he knows what their plight would be if left penniless in a frontier town.

Huck's basic knowledge of human nature is again illustrated when he knows that he can't tell Mary Jane the entire truth be-cause she is so honest that she would give it away by her looks and actions. Thus, again, he has to create a story and a plan which will take this fact into consideration.

CHAPTERS XXVII AND XXVIII

Summary

When Huck tries to leave the house with the money, he finds that he is locked inside. Fearing discovery, he shoves the bag of money under the coffin lid. He spends an uncomfortable night and has no opportunity to retrieve the money before the funeral.

The house is filled with people for the funeral sermon. When the undertaker finally screws the lid on the coffin, Huck is not sure whether the money is still inside or not. The next day, the king and the duke begin selling the Wilks property, including the slaves, claiming that it is necessary to return immediately to England, taking their nieces with them. The girls are overjoyed at the prospect.

On auction day, the king and the duke discover that the money is missing and they call Huck to account for it. Huck shifts the blame on the slaves, already sold, as he realizes that the sale is not valid and that the Negroes will be back in a week or two.

Huck encounters Mary Jane, weeping because of the separation of the slaves. Huck blurts out that the slaves will soon be returned and reunited. He makes Mary Jane promise to leave town for four days if he tells her why he knows that the slaves will be returned. When she promises, he reveals the entire hoax to her. She wishes to have the imposters tarred and feathered at once, but Huck reminds her of her promise to go away. He shortens the time to one day, asking her to put a candle in the window at eleven o'clock that night. If he does not come, she will know that he and the nameless other person whom he is shielding are gone; the spurious uncles can then be arrested and jailed. His purpose in sending her away is to keep her from betraying the secret through facial expressions.

Mary Jane promises to stand by Huck in case he should not escape. He advises her to use the "Royal Nonesuch" as proof of the rascality of the pair. He also writes a statement saying that he put the money in the coffin, but he makes her promise not to read it until she is on the way to the neighbor's home. She promises to pray for Huck. He explains her absence to the family by saying that she has gone to help a sick friend. While the sale is in progress, two more claimants of Peter Wilks' property arrive by steamboat.

Commentary

When *Huck Finn* first appeared, the book received some violent criticism for "violating" the taste and sensibility of the reading public. One of the scenes most often objected to was this one depicting the funeral. Critics found no humor in this "side-splitting account of a funeral, enlivened by a 'sick melodeum,' a 'long-legged undertaker,' and a rat episode in the cellar" (See *Life*, V, February 26, 1885). However, for the more sophisticated audience of today, Twain's description has become a classic. It is the first significant American satire on the sentimentality of funeral customs, ridiculing undertakers and all other aspects of burial customs.

The separation of families by the sale of slaves shows Huck's and Mary Jane's sense of humanity. The response is to the humanity of the Negroes and to the needless suffering. This response again prepares us for Huck's defense of Jim.

Huck's ability to lie successfully serves him well when he is confronted by the king and the duke about the stolen money. Without this ability, Huck's life would be in serious danger and he would be subjected to the brutality of the king and the duke. His conscience is not bothered by this lie because of the necessity of it. But in Chapter XXVIII, when he has to lie to Mary Jane, he considers for a moment the value of telling the truth: ". . . I'm blest if it don't look to me like the truth is better, and actuly *safer*, than a lie." But for Mary Jane's protection, he has to tell another lie. Furthermore, Huck's lying and his plan partly involve getting rid of the king and the duke so that he and Jim can continue on their odyssey without being hampered by others.

CHAPTERS XXIX AND XXX

Summary

The new set of Wilks brothers confront the king and duke, but when the handwriting of all four claimants is compared with that of letters written from England by Harvey Wilks, there are no satisfactory results. Then an argument arises about the tattoo marks on the dead man's chest, and it becomes necessary to exhume his body to find out. When the gold is discovered in the coffin, there is so much excitement that Huck is able to break loose from his captor and make a dash for the raft. Although he sees Mary Jane's candle in the window, he cannot stop until he rejoins Jim on the raft.

At first, Huck is happy to be back on the raft and to be free of the king and the duke, but soon he and Jim hear the rogues catching up with them in a canoe. Huck pacifies the king and duke by telling them that the man who had hold of him let him go and told him to run. The king and the duke argue with each other about the presence of the gold in the coffin, each blaming the other for planning to steal it later. Soon, however, the rogues make up their quarrel and become "thick as thieves" again.

Commentary

In Chapter XXIX, Twain uses an established comic technique — the confused identity of two sets of characters. This technique goes back to classical times. Thus in this chapter, we have a series of *tests* and the tests are conceived of in such a way as to provide humor and suspense. The suspense builds as each ruse devised to reveal the real identity of the people involved is thwarted in one manner or another. For example, the real William can't write because he has broken his right arm. Twain's magnificent narrative ability sustains the suspense.

It is ironic that when Huck is called upon to tell what he knows, Dr. Robinson tells him to sit down because he has had no practice in the art of lying. Of course, this is the first time that

Huck has had to lie to such an intelligent and honest man, and also the first time that he has had to lie when there was no practical reason for the lie.

The narrative plot is brought to its climax by the necessity of digging up the body to determine if there is a tattoo which would establish the real identity of the contesting uncles. This, therefore, reveals the presence of the gold and, while the townspeople are staring at the gold, Huck is able to make his escape.

At the end of Chapter XXIX, Huck's excitement and relief over escaping from the rogues and returning to Jim suggests the importance which he places on his relationship with Jim. But this relief is short-lived since the king and the duke escape their captors at the same time that Huck is fleeing.

In Chapter XXX, the scoundrels argue between themselves, each refusing to take the blame for the failure. In a rare insight, the duke reminds the king that they would have done the same thing to escape that Huck did. Thus, after the rogues' treachery with the Wilks, Twain tries to lessen their villainy somewhat so that we view them as believable characters rather than symbols of pure evil.

CHAPTER XXXI

Summary

For days and days, the king and the duke dare not let Huck and Jim stop at any town for fear of being detected. But when they consider themselves out of danger, they begin their old tricks of swindling again, but with small success. When they begin whispering to each other and talking confidentially, Huck and Jim become uneasy. One day the king goes ashore and sells Jim as a runaway slave for forty dollars. He then squanders the money without sharing it with the duke. Huck is indignant, claiming that Jim was *his* property and could not be sold without his permission. Huck then has a struggle with his conscience about returning Jim to Miss Watson, but his love for Jim is more important. Huck tears up the letter that he has written to Miss Watson, decides that he is willing to "go to hell" for Jim, and goes to search for Jim — determined to free him. He discovers that Jim is at the Phelps plantation not far away.

Commentary

Every detail and every scene has been leading up to this climactic chapter. By this time, both Huck and Jim are thoroughly fed up with the king and the duke, but are still afraid, physically and otherwise, of them. Jim is, after all, still a runaway slave and there are several indications that the king and the duke are aware of this.

The final calumny of the king and duke is selling Jim back into slavery. Even though Huck has known them to be the worse sort of scoundrels, his innocence does not allow him to foresee this ultimate treachery — to "make him a slave again . . . for forty dirty dollars." The horror for Huck lies partly in the reiterated fact that he is not overly concerned with money (he left $6000 in order to escape from Pap); to sell a human being such as Jim for "forty dirty dollars" is beyond Huck's understanding.

With the sale of Jim, Huck faces isolation and loneliness. Now, Huck is forced to come to terms with his own values, as opposed to the values of a society which would harbor such people as the rogues who sell Jim for forty dollars and the society which would buy him for that amount. Now he realizes the intrinsic worth of Jim as a human being and not as a piece of property to be bantered about at a sale.

In evaluating his position and coming to terms with this moral dilemma, Huck at first feels that his own behavior is at fault because he has helped a slave escape and that, consequently, he is being punished for this crime. He decides that "here was the plain hand of Providence slapping me in the face and letting me know my wickedness was being watched. . . ." Yet Huck cannot reconcile his own sense of personal wickedness with the needless torture of Jim.

Huck's attempt to pray is ironic and is a takeoff on *Hamlet*'s Claudius. But, unlike Claudius who can't pray because of his evil doings, Huck can't pray because his values are right, even though he can't realize that fact.

Accepting, as he has all along, that society is right and he is wrong, he can only ironically conclude that he is evil and, if his nature is aligned to evil, he might as well continue to live a life of wickedness. Thus, in deciding that he will "go to hell," he arrives at his momentous moral decision and decides that he will free Jim.

Huck's decision to "go to hell" is doubly ironic since we have seen Huck's higher moral sense in all the preceding scenes. Only in terms of the values of society has Huck done something wrong and, thus, we condemn society and embrace Huck's decision, even though he does not recognize his own moral superiority.

Immediately afterward, Huck encounters the duke and recognizes again their duplicity and fraudulence. At this time, however, Huck has no interest in making the rogues suffer for their action—his only concern is recovering Jim.

With the end of this chapter, in terms of formal structure, the second part of the novel—the experiences on the Mississippi River—comes to an end since the rest of the novel will take place on the Phelps plantation.

CHAPTERS XXXII AND XXXIII

Summary

When Huck arrives at the Phelps plantation, he hears the dim hum of a spinning wheel and a moment later is surrounded by dogs of all breeds and sizes. A Negro woman disperses them, and a white woman, followed by several small children, runs out and welcomes Huck, identifying herself as his Aunt Sally. Huck is at a loss to know who she is until Mr. Phelps appears and his wife introduces Huck as Tom Sawyer. To Huck, this is "like being born again" for he is now on familiar ground and can fabricate all kinds of stories about the Sawyer family.

On the way to town in a wagon, supposedly to bring back his baggage, Huck encounters Tom Sawyer. Tom has just alighted from a steamboat and thinks that he is seeing a ghost when the supposedly dead Huck appears. Huck confides his secret about Jim to Tom, who agrees to help the runaway slave gain freedom. Huck is astounded that Tom Sawyer would agree to such a horrible thing.

Tom puts on an act upon arrival, giving his name as William Thompson, from Ohio, looking for Mr. Archibald Nichols. He is told that Mr. Nichols lives three miles down the road, but that Tom must stay and eat with the family. Accepting the invitation, Tom at first offends Aunt Sally by kissing her but later is forgiven when he introduces himself as Sid Sawyer who had begged to come because Tom did.

After a meal large enough for seven families, the subject of the King's Cameleopard comes up. Huck and Tom try to warn the king and the duke that they are to be run out of town, but it is too late. The fraudulent two are tarred and feathered and ridden out of town on a rail.

Commentary

The basis of many of Huck's plans is found in his remark: "I went right along, not fixing up any particular plan, but just trusting to Providence to put the right words in my mouth when the time come." This practice has served Huck well so far in all the encounters throughout the book and now serves as a significant contrast to Tom Sawyer's elaborately contrived plots.

One objection which could be raised to this last section is the extreme coincidence in Jim's being sold to Tom Sawyer's aunt and uncle and the arrival of Huck Finn at the same time that

Tom Sawyer is expected and thus being taken for Tom. This co-incidence tests severely the credulity of the reader.

Huck's story about the boat blowing out a cylinder-head evokes the often criticized remark of Huck's in answering if any one was hurt: "No'm. Killed a nigger." Huck has apparently come to terms only with Jim and does not apply his new values to the entire black race. It is also worth noting that Aunt Sally, for all of her pious religion, apparently accepts the same view as does society about the fate of the Negroes.

The entire farcical tone of this last section is set by Aunt Sally herself as she has Huck hide from Uncle Silas. Because Aunt Sally delights in playing practical jokes, these types of pranks will be played on Aunt Sally herself and will characterize the tone of this last section.

The idea of death and rebirth is again utilized as Huck receives another new identity — this time as Tom Sawyer. The comic implication is that when he does meet Tom Sawyer, he is taken for a ghost. The explanation of his deeds seem insignificant in terms of the plans which Tom Sawyer plots. We should also compare Tom's surprise at seeing Huck with the lack of surprise in a later scene when Aunt Polly expresses no surprise, an apparent lapse on Twain's part.

When Huck tells Tom Sawyer that he plans to steal Jim out of bondage, Tom almost reveals that Jim is already free, a fact which is not revealed until the close of the novel, but one which the reader should keep in mind throughout all of the involved attempts to steal Jim. Furthermore, since Huck has always associated Tom with respectability, he is shocked that Tom is going to help steal Jim: "I'm bound to say Tom Sawyer fell, considerable, in my estimation. Only I couldn't believe it. Tom Sawyer a *nigger stealer!*" The point is that Huck is reconciled to being a wicked being, but Tom has always stood for moral correctness and social acceptance. Even in the first chapters, Tom requires a nickle to be left as payment when they "steal" a candle. However, in the total view, Tom is still the representative of socially correct behavior since he is *not* stealing Jim because Jim is already free.

The essential humanity that we saw in Huck is again illustrated when he sees the king and the duke tarred and feathered. In spite of the dirty trick which these scoundrels played on him, Huck is responsive to their suffering. Twain uses this scene as a comment against the "damned human race" by having Huck say: "It was a dreadful thing to see. Human beings *can* be awful cruel to one another." However, one objection to this last part is that Huck, basically sensitive to the sufferings of others, allows Jim to suffer insensitively while effecting the plan for Jim's escape. In contrast, however, it has been argued that Jim allows these tricks and indignities to be perpetrated against him.

CHAPTERS XXXIV, XXXV, AND XXXVI

Summary

Tom Sawyer discovers that Jim is a prisoner in a hut behind the house. The two boys discuss plans of freeing their friend, but Tom finds Huck's plan too simple. Tom favors something more elaborate than stealing the key, unlocking the door of the hut, and taking Jim down the river on a raft. The boys must dig Jim out using the complicated methods of adventure tales. The Negro in charge of Jim is made to believe that witches are haunting him when Jim unwittingly speaks words of recognition to Huck and Tom.

Tom's dark, deep-laid plans include digging a tunnel, sawing off the leg of the bed to which Jim is chained, using a rope-ladder, having Jim break out a window that is flimsily secured, and a variety of other invented difficulties. Tom cites examples from his reading, proving how the job should be done. Huck is overwhelmed by Tom's erudition and superior grasp of the subject. Willingly, Huck steals a sheet, a shirt, and some case-knives for use in the great liberation of Jim. The boys have to make haste because Mr. Phelps will soon hear from New Orleans that Jim did not come from there and will probably learn the truth.

Digging with case-knives proves so slow and laborious that Tom finally consents to use picks and pretend that they are case-knives. Dog-tired, he is unable to climb the lightning rod to the second story and yields to Huck's suggestion to "let on" that the stairway is a lightning rod. The boys in various ways acquire and smuggle in such articles as a pewter spoon, a chopped-up brass candlestick, and three tin plates to assist in the great plan of escape, in addition to the rope ladder and the white shirt on which Jim is to record his experiences in blood. Tom says that this is the best fun he has ever had in his life. Jim's Negro keeper, Nat, is to deliver the witch-pie, containing a rope ladder made of a sheet torn in strips.

Commentary

In the presence of Tom Sawyer, Huck becomes less self-sufficient. He loses that sense of independence which he possessed on the raft and in earlier episodes. He is, however, still shrewd enough to know that any plan which he might suggest would not be good enough for Tom Sawyer. In showing the contrast between Huck's plan and Tom's plan, Twain is continuing the contrast between Huck's natural common sense as opposed to the bookish artificiality of Tom's absurd plans based upon romantic fiction. Throughout these chapters, Twain is ridiculing the then-current popularity of romantic fiction whose pages were filled with daring escapes and thrilling adventures.

Huck's main conflict in these chapters is that of having to choose and follow the absurd plans of Tom Sawyer, which were conceived for their "style" and "artistic value," rather than following his own innate sense of what was practical. As Tom continues to allow Jim to suffer in order to effect his ridiculous plan, we see again that the respectable element of society is often oblivious to the suffering of the human being.

Tom's respectability is emphasized mainly to make the above contrast. For example, Tom forces Huck to pay a dime for the watermelon he stole, but at the same time he has no human feeling for Jim's suffering. His respectability becomes more cruel when we realize that Jim's freedom has already been given to him, yet Tom Sawyer's plans keep Jim in bondage, thereby making Tom Sawyer directly responsible not for the freeing of Jim but for the enslavement of Jim. Thus, for the sake of romantic style, Tom keeps a free man in prison simply to satisfy his own sense of personal achievement. With this view in mind, these episodes lose a great deal of the humor inherent in the escapades.

The use of superstition is continued, but now it loses much of its humor. For example, Tom and Huck have convinced the slave Nat that he sees witches and, by this ruse, they are able to carry out many of their plans. But while they are convincing Nat that there are no dogs in Jim's cabin, Jim is suffering from having bitten into the corn-pone with the concealed candlestick which "most mashed his teeth out." Humor ceases to be funny when it involves actual physical pain, but Tom Sawyer is not concerned with the suffering of others as long as his plan is done with style. Additionally, however, Tom is not later concerned with even his *own* suffering because of the gun shot; the plan was carried out with such style that nothing else matters.

CHAPTERS XXXVII, XXXVIII, AND XXXIX

Summary

Soon, Aunt Sally begins to miss things that have disappeared, including a shirt, a spoon, and six candles. One servant adds a sheet to the list of missing articles and another reports a brass candlestick. Uncle Silas sheepishly produces a spoon from his pocket, where, without his knowledge, Tom has put it. The boys have to acquire another spoon and are able to do so right under Aunt Sally's nose. They drop it in her apron pocket, and Jim takes it out, as prearranged. So confused does she become eventually that she cannot remember her original number of sheets, shirts, and spoons.

Making pens out of candlesticks and saws out of case-knives proves slow and tedious, and it takes Huck and Tom three weeks to collect rats, snakes, spiders, shirts, spoons, and other equipment necessary for the freeing of Jim in grand style. The Phelps household is in constant turmoil, as the rats and snakes get loose and frighten the occupants, especially Aunt Sally. Jim, who has to endure the spiders, rats, and delays says that if he ever gets out this time, he will never be a prisoner again, not for any salary. He is supposed to produce captive's tears with an onion and to write on the shirt with blood drawn when the rats bite him. An anonymous letter, Tom's idea, warns the family and their friends that a *"desprate gang of cutthroats from over in the Ingean Territory"* is going to steal Jim that night.

Commentary

If we could forget the serious implications of keeping Jim imprisoned, then these chapters involving the preparations for the escape could be seen as in the best tradition of the frontier tall tale, filled with all sorts of exaggerations. The only alleviating factor in the perverse cruelty to Jim is the fact that Jim allows these things to be done—and even participates in some of the antics. We must remember that Jim knows and trusts both Huck and Tom and, therefore, consents to the antics even though he could at any time effect his own escape.

With these thoughts in mind, one can read these chapters for their preposterous scheme with all the gaudy details. In other words, the intellectual implications are somewhat obscured by the very fantastic nature of Tom's plans. The rendering of the frontier, religious household, filled with snakes, rats, spiders, and frogs, is a comic scene which overrides many of the intellectual objections.

Yet, the very comic aspect of these schemes is somewhat modified by the horror which they cause other people. Aunt Sally is, after all, a kind and generous person in most ways, and her undue fears and painful experiences cause these episodes to lose some of their comic value. For Tom Sawyer, his plans and his own satisfactions overrule any consideration for others and, for this reason, Tom must be seen as a rather self-centered boy who subjects not just Jim—but anyone—to cruel tricks for his own sense of personal gratification. Furthermore, Tom's letter, which threatens a raid by outlaws, was more serious than he realizes since a raid by outlaws is a real threat to people living on the edge of the frontier.

These chapters also illuminate the characters of Aunt Sally, dictatorial but generous of heart, and Uncle Silas, hen-pecked but good natured. It is only when we take the larger view that we see that both, in spite of their pious religious mouthings, are still anxious to get the reward for Jim and, this failing, they will sell him on the open market. Their view, then, is the same as society's view. It becomes even more paradoxical when we realize that these "good Christians" are very concerned with teaching Christianity to Jim before they sell him.

CHAPTERS XL AND XLI

Summary

On the night of Jim's escape, Huck and Tom get up at half-past eleven and begin eating a lunch they stole. Tom sends Huck to the basement to get some butter, and Huck is caught by Aunt Sally and sent into the "setting-room." There he sees fifteen farmers with guns, all prepared for the desperate men from the Indian Territory. As soon as Huck can slip away, he joins Tom and Jim in the hut, and the three escape, as planned, through the hole. Tom gets caught on a splinter, which snaps and makes a noise. In a moment, bullets and dogs pursue them. The three get away, but not before Tom is shot in the leg.

Tom is proud of his wound and insists on bandaging it himself. Huck and Jim consult, however, and agree that Tom must have a doctor. Huck is to go for one, and Jim is to hide in the woods until the doctor is gone again.

After Huck tells the doctor a convincing story, the doctor takes Huck's canoe and goes to tend to Tom. Huck is discovered by Uncle Silas, and he hears how worried Aunt Sally is over them. When they get back to the plantation, there are many exaggerated versions of what really happened. Aunt Sally tells Huck that she is not going to lock the doors but relies upon him not to run away again. Because of her kindness to him, Huck stays in his room that night.

Commentary

High melodrama takes over in the lurid account of the liberation of Jim, replete with blood hounds, gun-toting men, an escape through a secret tunnel in the presence of the posse, and a wild gunshot which wounds Tom. Thus Tom's foolishness and devotion to "style" leads to real danger, one that could have cost Jim his life. Tom is punished by being shot, but his wound will later be a source of great pleasure when he wears the bullet around his neck.

With Tom wounded and the "mixed-up en splendid" plan completed, Huck takes over and returns to his practical planning. To effect the plan to help Tom, Jim has to lose his freedom again. His sacrifice restores the innate dignity to him that he was deprived of during the wild schemes of Tom Sawyer. Jim's anxiety over Tom and his willingness to risk his hard-earned freedom — and even his life — to procure a doctor for the wounded Tom shows Jim's unselfishness and basic response to humanity in contrast to the selfishness of Tom and his desire for a successful, stylistic escape.

In getting the doctor, Huck ignores Tom's instructions and makes up a simple, believable story in order to get the doctor to come to Tom. Ironically, had Huck followed Tom's advice, Tom would probably have died of the gunshot wound. No longer under the influence of Tom Sawyer, Huck reverts to the type of behavior which characterized him during the earlier parts of the novel. And finally, after all of the trouble which Tom Sawyer has caused Aunt Sally, Huck's compassion for her reaffirms his superiority to Tom Sawyer.

CHAPTER XLII AND CHAPTER THE LAST

Summary

When Tom is brought home the next morning on a mattress, he is delirious. Jim is at once captured and chained again in the cabin, with a guard on duty at all times. The doctor intervenes in Jim's behalf, however, and explains how unselfish Jim's conduct has been.

Aunt Sally concentrates on nursing Tom back to health. When he regains consciousness, he explains to her the whole elaborate procedure for freeing Jim, the "nonnamous" letter and how much fun it all was. She has never heard of the likes and can hardly believe that these "little rapscallions" are responsible for it all. She promises to punish Tom when he is well enough. Tom sits up in bed and makes the startling announcement that Jim was already set free two months ago by Miss Watson's will. The whole escapade was planned for adventure only. At this point, Aunt Polly arrives from St. Petersburg and greets her sister, Aunt Sally. The identity of Tom, posing as Sid, and Huck, pretending to be Tom, is at last revealed.

Jim is out of chains in no time and Tom gives him forty dollars for being such a patient prisoner. Jim finally reveals that the dead man in the floating house was Pap. Tom is proud of his wound and wears the bullet around his neck. Huck, however, feels that it is time for him to head out for new territory because Aunt Sally wants to adopt him and "sivilize" him and he can't stand that again.

Commentary

These final two chapters resolve the fantastic mistaken identity and clear matters up for Jim. Huck is able once again to reclaim his own name and become his real self once more.

In Chapter XLII, Jim is about to be killed as an example to other Negroes who try to run off; what saves him, however, is man's fear of destroying someone else's property and thus being financially in debt for the lynching. Yet, the doctor attests to the goodness of Jim and, instead of killing him, the good, decent Phelps merely locks him up and keeps him "on bread and water, and loaded down with chains. . . ."

When Tom hears that Jim is again imprisoned, he reveals that Jim has been free all this time. This revelation is partly due to his disappointment that his fantastic scheme to free Jim did not work. This revelation, however, is totally unmotivated. There is no indication earlier in the novel that someone like Miss Watson could undergo such a transformation as to actually free Jim. Instead, her type and her society represent everything that Jim and Huck were trying to escape from. But most critics tend to overlook some of these flaws as Twain's attempt to bring the novel to a rapid ending. With this revelation, Huck can finally understand why someone like Tom Sawyer could actually help "set a nigger free." Huck now realizes the hypocrisy of Tom's actions and now that he has his own name back, he recaptures some of those qualities which were suppressed when he assumed Tom's name.

In the last chapter, Twain returns to Jim's superstitions. Jim had predicted earlier that he would be rich and, now that he owns himself, he feels that he is now a rich man. In contrast, however, Huck feels that his pap has probably drunk up all of the money that Huck had. This fear necessitates Jim's revealing that Pap is dead. The mere fact that when Huck learns this and says nothing, nor shows any regret, indicates his lack of concern over the welfare of his worthless pap.

The novel ends as it began. In the second paragraph of Chapter I, Huck feared that the Widow Douglas would try to "sivilize" him and, at the end of the novel, he feels the need to escape again because this time Aunt Sally wants to adopt him and "sivilize" him. And throughout the novel, we have seen that Huck functions as a much nobler person when he is not confined by the hypocrisy of civilization.

CHARACTER ANALYSES

HUCK FINN

Huck Finn is one of America's best-loved fictional characters. Critically, he has been the subject of numerous studies and interpretations, many of them so unique as to make Huck unrecognizable.

Since Huck is the narrator of a book filled with humor, it is highly significant that we recognize that Huck himself has no sense of humor; in fact, he is almost totally literal minded. For example, he can see no humor in the age-old joke about where Moses was when the lights went out. It is inconceivable to him that the drunk riding the horse at the circus is really a highly trained acrobat. For a while, he literally believes a genie can be made to appear by rubbing an old lamp.

Since Huck is so completely literal minded, he therefore makes a superb narrator in that he tells or reports everything he sees or hears with straightforward accuracy. He never exaggerates or embroiders on anything he narrates and, therefore, we can always trust Huck's account or narration of any event to be realistic.

Huck possesses most of the qualities which are necessary for life on the frontier. He is always practical and natural, exhibiting good common sense except in such rare episodes as the snake episode. Furthermore, Huck is extremely adaptable. He can learn to tolerate living with the Widow Douglas and then can quickly transform his ways to that of living in the wilderness, or on a raft, or in the "so-called" elegance of the Grangerfords. Huck's adaptability, then, allows him to function well in different types of situations.

Huck is also very shrewd and possesses a good inventive ability. On the frontier, a man had to be shrewd to survive many situations. Thus, Huck is shrewd enough to be able to determine what motivates such people as the "bounty hunters" and then is inventive enough to create a story which is so credible that he and Jim are left alone.

Huck is also a person who responds sympathetically to other human beings. He tries to save the cutthroats on the *Walter Scott,* he saves the king and the duke from a posse and later even feels sorry for them when they are tarred and feathered, and he responds deeply to the plight of the Wilks girls. This is the same quality which allows him to appreciate and love Jim.

Huck's sympathy for other human beings, his shrewdness and ingenuity, his basic intelligence, his good common sense and his basic practicality — these are among the qualities which make Huck Finn one of the great characters in American fiction.

JIM

Along with Huck, Jim is the other major figure in the novel. One of his primary functions is to act as a gauge for Huck's development. In other words, while Huck knows Jim in St. Petersburg, it is not until Jackson's Island and the trip down the river that Huck learns to appreciate Jim's great worth as a human being.

At first, Jim is seen only as a person who is filled with superstitions, but once on the island, we discover that many of his superstitions are based upon good common sense, practicality, and a knowledge of natural surroundings. Gradually, on the trip down the river, we begin to see many other fine attributes such as his unselfish and towering love for his family, his dedication and love for Huck and, later, even his love for Tom Sawyer.

Jim's willingness to sacrifice himself for others and take on Huck's duties as they float down the river causes Huck to see Jim's basic worth. As he begins to accept Jim as a human being, he becomes aware of Jim's sense of love and humanity, his basic goodness, and his desire to help others. These qualities, then, force Huck into his decision to "go to hell" for Jim.

TOM SAWYER

In contrast to the individuality of Huck Finn and his rejection of the values of society, Tom Sawyer represents the values of the society from which Huck is escaping and also a conformity to those values. On a superficial level, it would appear that Tom Sawyer is the more imaginative of the two, but Tom's oaths, his schemes, and his escapades are based upon books about romantic adventures which he has read. Whereas Huck has the ability and shrewdness to function outside of society, Tom Sawyer would founder. Huck is involved in real life and Tom functions only when he is imitating something which he has read in a book. Tom's plans are always extravagant, absurd, or ridiculous while Huck's are simple, practical and shrewd.

Tom's conformity is seen in such events as when he makes Huck leave a nickle on the table for the candles, or when he makes Huck pay for the watermelon. These small facts lend credence to Huck's view that Tom Sawyer could not possibly help free a slave in the last section of the novel because of Tom's respectability and conformity to the views of his society.

REVIEW QUESTIONS

1. Compare and contrast the characters and personalities of Tom Sawyer and Huck Finn.

2. Choose several episodes from along the Mississippi River and show how each contributes to Huck's education.

3. In writing a humorous book, why does Twain have a narrator who has no sense of humor?

72

4. Discuss the principal function of the river in this novel.

5. Discuss the role of superstition in this novel.

6. Many critics have objected to the episodes at the Phelps plantation. What could be some of the objections?

7. Lionel Trilling says that Jim is Huck's "true father." Defend or refute this statement.

8. Discuss the differences between the freedom of the raft and the restrictions of society on the shore.

9. If the purpose of the trip down the Mississippi is to gain freedom for Jim, why do they continue deeper and deeper into slave territory?

10. Huck has been accused of knowing more than a fourteen-year-old boy could possibly know. Citing specific material from the novel, discuss this statement.

SELECTED BIBLIOGRAPHY

BELLAMY, GLADYS CARMEN. *Mark Twain as a Literary Artist.* Norman: University of Oklahoma Press, 1950.

BLAIR, WALTER. *Mark Twain and Huck Finn.* Berkeley: University of California Press, 1960.

DEVOTO, BERNARD. *Mark Twain at Work.* Cambridge: Harvard University Press, 1942.

FERGUSON, DELANCEY. *Mark Twain: Man and Legend.* Indianapolis: The Bobbs-Merrill Company, 1943.

LEARY, LEWIS. *Mark Twain.* Minneapolis: University of Minnesota Press, 1959.

LONG, E. HUDSON. *Mark Twain Handbook.* New York: Hendricks House, 1957.

MARX, LEO. "Mr. Eliot, Mr. Trilling, and *Huckleberry Finn.*" *American Scholar,* XXII (Autumn, 1953), 423-40.

ROURKE, CONSTANCE. *American Humor: A Study of the National Character.* New York: Harcourt, Brace & Company, Inc. 1931, pp. 209-20.

SALOMON, ROGER B. *Twain and the Image of History.* New Haven: Yale University Press, 1961.

SCOTT, ARTHUR L., ed. *Mark Twain: Selected Criticism.* Dallas: Southern Methodist University Press, 1955.

STONE, ALBERT E., JR. *The Innocent Eye: Childhood in Mark Twain's Imagination.* New Haven: Yale University Press, 1961.

NOTES

Do You Know Someone Special?

Cliffs Speech and Hearing Series can help with many special education problems

This series of up-to-date overviews helps you quickly become familiar with areas of special education. As a student, teacher or concerned individual, these easy-to-follow presentations also give you helpful definition of terms, glossary and an annotated bibliography.

ORDER BLANK   QTY.

1816-0	Aphasia ($3.95)	
1810-1	Articulation Disorders; Methods of Evaluation and Therapy ($3.95)	
1830-6	Auditory Processing and Learning Disabilities ($3.95)	
1813-6	Basic Audiometry — Including Impedance Measurement ($4.95)	
1819-5	Cerebral Palsy: Speech, Hearing, and Language Problems ($3.95)	
1801-2	Cleft Palate and Associated Speech Characteristics ($4.95)	
1803-9	Clinical Management of Voice Disorders ($4.95)	
1826-8	Hearing Impairment Among Aging Persons ($2.75)	
1832-2	Language Disorders in Adolescents	
1828-4	Speech-Hearing Pathology and Surgery ($4.95)	
1807-1	Speech and Hearing Problems in the Classroom ($3.95)	
1805-5	Stuttering: What It Is and What To Do About It ($3.95)	
1822-5	Tongue Thrust ($3.95)	

Name _____

Address _____

City _____

State _____ Zip _____

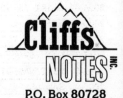

P.O. Box 80728
Lincoln, NE 68501

Your Guides to Successful Test Preparation.

Cliffs Test Preparation Guides

Efficient preparation means better test scores. Go with the experts and use Cliffs Test Preparation Guides. They'll help you reach your goals because they're: • Complete • Concise • Functional • In-depth. They are focused on helping you know what to expect from each test. The test-taking techniques have been proven in classroom programs nationwide.

Recommended for individual use or as a part of formal test preparation programs.

Available at your local bookseller or order by sending the coupon with your check.

Cliffs Notes, P.O. Box 80728, Lincoln, NE 68501

	TITLES	QTY.
2004-1	ACT ($4.95)	
2030-0	CBEST ($6.95)	
1471-8	ESSAY EXAM ($2.95)	
2016-5	GED Mathematics ($3.95)	
2014-9	GED Reading Skills ($2.95)	
2010-6	GED Science ($3.95)	
2012-2	GED Social Studies ($3.95)	
2015-7	GED Writing Skills ($3.95)	
2006-8	GMAT ($5.95)	
2008-4	GRE ($5.95)	
2021-1	LSAT ($5.95)	
2017-3	NTE ($9.95)	
2002-5	PSAT/NMSQT ($3.25)	
2000-9	SAT ($4.95)	
2018-1	TOEFL ($14.95)	

Prices subject to change without notice.

Name_____

Address_____

City_____

State _____ Zip_____

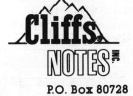

P.O. Box 80728
Lincoln, NE 68501

Here's a Great Way to Study Shakespeare and Chaucer.

Cliffs Complete Study Editions

These easy-to-use volumes contain everything that a student or teacher needs for an individual classic. Each attractively illustrated volume includes abundant biographical, historical and literary background information. A descriptive bibliography provides guidance in the selection of additional reading.

The inviting three-column arrangement offers the maximum in convenience to the reader. Shakespeare's plays are presented in a full, authoritative text with modern spelling. Each line of Chaucer's original poetry is followed by a literal translation in simple current English. Adjacent to the complete text, there is a running commentary that gives clear supplementary discussion. Obscure words and allusions are keyed by line number and clarified opposite to where they occur.

COMPLETE STUDY EDITIONS	QTY.
SHAKESPEARE	
Hamlet	
Julius Caesar	
King Henry IV, Part 1	
King Lear	
Macbeth	
The Merchant of Venice	
Othello	
Romeo and Juliet	
The Tempest	
Twelfth Night	
CHAUCER'S CANTERBURY TALES	
The Prologue	
The Wife of Bath	

Prices subject to change without notice.

$3.95 each

Available at your booksellers or send this form with your check or money order to Cliffs Notes.

Name _____

Address _____

City _____

State _____ Zip _____

P.O. Box 80728
Lincoln, NE 68501

Make Your Best Score on these important tests...

Get Cliffs Test Preparation Guides

Full-length practice tests — explanatory answers — self-scoring charts let you analyze your performance.

Explains successful approaches to the four basic test areas: English, mathematics, social studies and natural science.

Good scores on this test can help you earn your scholarship — it also gives you extra practice for the SAT. Know what to expect, and do your best!

An easy-to-use book that is valuable not only for essay examinations but as a guide for effective writing.

Available at your local bookseller or send in your check with the coupon below.
Cliffs Notes, Inc., P.O. Box 80728, Lincoln, NE 68501

- -

TITLES	QTY.
Cliffs ACT Preparation Guide ($4.95)	
Cliffs ESSAY EXAM Preparation Guide ($2.95)	
Cliffs PSAT/NMSQT Preparation Guide ($3.25)	
Cliffs SAT Preparation Guide ($4.95)	

Name_____

Address_____

City_____

State _____ Zip_____

P.O. Box 80728
Lincoln, NE 68501